HOW
TO
SUCCEED
IN
HIGH
SCHOOL

HOW TO SUCCEED IN HIGH SCHOOL

Second Edition

Barbara Mayer

VGM Career Horizons
NTC/Contemporary Publishing Group

Library of Congress Cataloging-in-Publication Data

Mayer, Barbara, 1939–
    How to succeed in high school / Barbara Mayer.—2nd ed.
      p.   cm.
   ISBN 0-8442-2941-5
    1. High school students—Handbooks, manuals, etc.   2. High
schools—Handbooks, manuals, etc.   I. Title.
LB3605
373.18—dc21   99-23655
                                             CIP

Published by VGM Career Horizons
A division of NTC/Contemporary Publishing Group, Inc.
4255 West Touhy Avenue, Lincolnwood (Chicago), Illinois 60712-1975 U.S.A.
Copyright © 2000, 1990 by NTC/Contemporary Publishing Group, Inc.
Printed in the United States of America
International Standard Book Number: 0-8442-2941-5

00 01 02 03 04 05 CU 15 14 13 12 11 10 9 8 7 6 5 4 3 2 1

There are two marks of a strong individual—
how well he learns,
and how well he teaches.

For Edward Klapak

Knowledge shared is
knowledge expanded. Thanks for the sharing!

Contents

Introduction

This new edition of *How to Succeed in High School* discusses many of the problems you face as a teen. Some of the sections may hit a bit too close to home, but you deserve all the good advice you can get, and that's what this book is for.

These are not easy days for anyone. The first years of a new century, let alone a new millennium, give people of all ages reason to pause and consider where they are now, as well as where they are going. As a teenager now, you can look forward to many years of growth and experience. The trick is getting through these formative years, and understanding where you are, so you'll have a better idea of where you're going.

Whether you are new to the high school scene or well on your way to graduation, this book can help if you let it. More than getting through high school successfully, these pages give you a chance to learn more about yourself. They are full of help on how to understand yourself better, and give you opportunities to face your own feelings and thoughts as you analyze situations, attitudes, and problems that concern you.

This book doesn't involve homework, but it does include some exercises designed to help you know yourself better. The topic of this book isn't anything else but you, as well as all the challenges and opportunities you face. This is a book, however, and not a television channel. It involves some work on your part, but it promises to help make a more aware, confident, and successful you!

Read carefully, and learn as much as you can about who you are. Then you can succeed at the art of living as the best teenager and young adult you can be.

Understanding Yourself 1

If Kermit the Frog felt it isn't easy being green, you may take heart in the fact it isn't easy being a teen, either. There you sit—a special and unique person. What makes you so special? For one thing, by picking up this book you have admitted two very good things about yourself:

1. You want to know more about yourself, and

2. You have at least a vague desire to make your life during these high school years a better one.

You are saying, "Teach me something I don't know," and that makes you one of the healthiest and potentially most terrific people around!

Many people complain about high school, but most sane people will admit it is an interesting and consequential part of anyone's life. During these four years, you will be asked to make as many decisions as a United Nations member. You will probably do as much work as a U.N. member, too, and you may have to listen to more boring speeches!

Your high school years are a time when you, and many aspects of your life, are changing. These are the years when the adult "you" begins to take definite form. By the time you pick up that diploma and head for your first graduation party, the world will expect you to be capable of handling most jobs, most problems, and most responsibilities of adult life.

That's a big order. So as you sit down to try and make the most of these years, the first place to begin is getting to know and appreciate yourself. You are not a carbon copy of your brothers or sisters. You're not what your parents think you are. You're not even what your best friend thinks you are.

And even the "real you" is changing as you become an adult. Each decision you make now contributes a great deal to the person you're becoming.

You're on your way; now it's a matter of living the next few years as well as you can.

The Beauty of Being Human

One sure thing you have on your side as you tackle teenage life is the fact you are human. Everyone makes mistakes, has emotions and dreams, and shares the same concerns about living. Circumstances change at different ages, but the one thing all adults realize about you is that you are basically good, as they are. You have potential and ambition, as they do, and you share the same faults and possible talents. You also have the luxury of more time to get it all right.

The problem for many teens is simply understanding these facts themselves. Adolescence is a pressure-packed time. The very word sounds more like a disease than a time of life. Parents and teachers keep addressing the matter of success or failure, and teens can get so caught up in the hassle of meeting requirements they forget to pay attention to their own humanity.

Facing the high school years becomes much easier if you understand yourself. Others may set goals for you and expect certain things from you, but you are the one who must be true to yourself. You're the one who has the task of making the most of yourself and your future.

No Small Change

One of the first things to understand about yourself is that you are changing. A lot of adults, and some who may be making your life miserable, have never really understood that life moves. Times and people change. Part of the human condition is to move and change, too.

The world of nature has evolved over millions of years. Scientists say chickens used to have large wings. Modern chickens have no use for them, however, and the wing has slowly become an insignificant part of the chicken's body. Just try making a meal of one chicken wing!

People also evolve during their lifetimes. There are many things you did and felt as a child. Now they are inconsequential because your life has moved into a different, more complex stage. One great secret that you should begin to understand is that this evolutionary process is still going on, and will continue as long as you live.

Rapping It Up

The first important concept in understanding yourself is to recognize and be comfortable with your own personal development. Others in your life may not be so quick to notice and respond to the changes. Parents are notorious for not realizing their children have reached a certain age and a certain level of development. Just when your folks have learned to cope with you at fourteen, your fifteenth birthday has rolled around, and you are already moving to new levels of awareness and maturity. This, of course, is one of the causes for the famous generation gap.

One simple answer is to recognize and respond to the changes in yourself. Once you are sure of these changes in your values, your interests, and your perspective, it is easier for others in your life to be aware of them, too.

Points to Ponder

1. What do you consider your most important change over the past year?

_____

_____

Why is it so important to you?

_____

_____

2. What changes in yourself do you feel others have failed to notice?

_____

_____

Why do you think they haven't noticed the change?

_____

3. What is important to you now that wasn't very important to you last year at this time?

_____

_____

What do you think this change says about you? Is it positive or negative?

_____

_____

4. Name two things that may be keeping you from really liking who you are right now.

_____

_____

Values and Priorities

Social studies teachers are famous for requiring students to learn who discovered what, and when. Knowing such facts may make your report card less traumatic and win some points on the home front, but the most important discovery you can make during your teens is who you are, and who you are becoming.

"Great," you say. "But how can I do it?"

First, look at the things that are important in your life. What you value, what is high on your list of priorities, says a lot about you. What gives you pleasure? Is it having a closet full of clothes and the best sound equipment this side of Jupiter? Is it your family? Is it knowing you have good friends who can be trusted and who will be there when you need them? Is it taking a quiet walk by yourself and just listening to the world going by? What is most important to you—making the honor roll, or hanging out with your friends?

Although you may not want to take the time, it would help if you calmly sit down and make a list of the things you value. That will give you a good idea of who you are now, and who you're possibly becoming. True, there are many facets to your life at this point, and they all need attention. But what you value most will take your best effort and most of your time. By looking at where you are putting your energy, you can begin to realize certain directions your life is taking. That realization will give you a better understanding of yourself.

Believing Is Seeing

What you believe is also a key factor in your identity. And the other side of that coin is just as important. What you choose not to believe will affect the way you respond to many circumstances that come along. It will set patterns that may last the rest of your life.

For example, if your religious beliefs are important to you, many decisions you make will find their source in these convictions. If, on the other hand, you are not strongly influenced by religion, you may have to look for other areas of security. You may need to find some working alternatives for religious guidelines and principles of living.

If you feel loved by your family, home and family responsibilities may be important to you. Or, getting out of the house may be one of your most sought-after pleasures, and the time you spend there may too often be filled with tension and frustration. If so, you should be aware your own attitudes toward marriage and family life may be developing in negative ways. You will not become a carbon copy of your parents. You are on your own track of development, and you can make the changes now that will lead to the parent and adult you want to be.

If you have trouble honestly loving the people who have shared all of your life with you, you may have to set some priorities straight and get things back into perspective before you launch out to find the one and only who will "really understand." What you believe and what you love are two of the most basic things about you. By honestly analyzing these two aspects of your life, you can learn a lot about yourself and begin to make any changes you think are in order.

Decisions! Decisions!

Another tip-off to your own identity lies in looking at the choices you make. There is only so much time in each day, and you have limited energy. What you decide to do, or not do, stems directly from your values and priorities and shows the direction you are headed.

If making the honor roll is the be-all and end-all of your life, and your parents demand nothing less than A's, you may find yourself putting in extra study time instead of taking a few hours to do things you enjoy. The pressure for grades is intense for some teens, and because of it, some students neglect other aspects of their lives.

Work is fine. It is part of the human condition and should be a serious concern in everyone's life. When, however, the need to succeed in one area begins to overshadow the greater success that comes from being a well-rounded and balanced person, it's time to realign priorities and learn to keep things in perspective. Putting all your apples in one cart may sound like a good idea, but the world does not live by apple pie alone!

You may be smiling at this point. "Never fear," you say. "Don't worry about me spending too much time with the books!" You may even be so caught up in your image at school that you won't volunteer the right answer when you know it, just so others won't think you're an egghead.

In this case, the decisions and choices you make are yours. They tell you, and the rest of the world, what you care about, what you are, and what you want to be. They also tell you how much importance you place on other people's opinions of you.

Your Place in the Group

Another good way to understand more about who you really are is to analyze how you react to situations.

A teacher sets up a group project in class and turns students loose on a particular topic. This project calls for understanding of basic principles, some ideas to get it going, and then a course of action.

As soon as the group gets settled, Steve immediately starts talking. He begins to set things in motion. He is a natural leader, and when something needs to get done, he takes charge and gets everyone else working. He is the spark plug, the initiator, and because of his intangible leadership quality, others follow him. Even though they may challenge him on certain points or not like his way of taking charge, they accept him as the leader.

Julie, on the other hand, sits back a while. She is the thinker. While everyone else is busy getting preliminary discussion out of the way, she is quietly sizing up the big picture. When her time comes, she may say very little, but her ideas will be the most workable. The suggestions she makes will form the basis for the whole project.

Once the work begins, Darren will jump in, volunteering to handle one aspect of the project. He may not be the person who comes up with the ideas, but he is a doer. Where he shines is in taking the ball and running with it. Because he may not be sure enough of himself to propose new ideas, Darren is a follower. He is the one who does most of the actual work, and he does it well. Once he understands where the project is going, he sets his own goals and does the work necessary to achieve them. People like Darren are often the ones who succeed in their adult lives, because they know how to actually make things happen, rather than just leave them in the idea stage.

Over on the fringe of the group sits Kathy. Ah, Kathy! At this point in her life, Kathy is still very much a spectator. She is too unsure of herself and her abilities, so she chooses to stay in the background. She watches others participate, and she avoids any possible confrontations. Her time will come, and she will become involved when others demand it. Her choice, however, is to remain on the sidelines and let everyone else handle things.

What would you do if you were part of this group? Are you a natural leader like Steve, or are you more like Kathy? Notice how you act in group situations, and you will have another important clue to your true self.

Recent studies on right-brained and left-brained people may also help. Left-brained people tend to be more methodical in their action-oriented way, while right-brained people may do better in considering possibilities. Taking some of the popular tests available on the Internet and through other sources can give you a better understanding of how your mind works.

Try to remember the last time you took part in a group activity. Were you an achiever, a leader, an idea person, a follower, a key worker, or a spectator? Write your answer here, with some reasons for your decision.

_____

_____

_____

_____

The "In" Crowd

Kathy is not the only one who may choose to sit back and spectate. There is another type of person who may sit on the sidelines, simply because that's where he or she feels safe. As high school groups and cliques develop—and they certainly will—one group of students becomes the "in" clique in school. While a certain amount of popularity is great, and everyone needs friends, some members of the "in" clique develop some strange characteristics.

Some of the people in this group become so secure they feel they never have to try for anything. They may be physically attractive, or they may have personalities that win over teachers and authority figures. They may come from wealthier or more connected families, or have other advantages most people do not. What can happen to them, however, is they may get everything too easily. They don't really *do* anything; they just *are* popular.

But some of these students don't really work hard at anything; they have a tendency to let any group down when work needs to be done. Why? They may not know how to follow a project through because they've never had to do it. As a result, they may add their presence to your group, but little more.

Are these words a bit hard on popular people? Maybe. But it's often true. And sadly, some high school superstars don't succeed much after high school. They get in the groove of simply being part of the right crowd and using that popularity as success. In later life, when work and the ability to follow through are essential to getting and keeping a good job, these people are often missing many of the basic skills others learned the hard way in high school. Don't let yourself use popularity as a substitute for hard work.

Of course, many popular people do find lasting success. The answer is simply not being satisfied with knowing you're on the inside, where most others would love to be.

Learn to work and follow through, and you can achieve goals that last far beyond the fleeting high school years.

Roles Aren't Everything

Our world has become very specialized and role-oriented. When people meet, one of the first questions is usually, "What do you do for a living?"

What we do, our job, seems to be an easy way for others to put us in perspective. While this is all right to a point, there is a great danger of confusing our different roles with our basic identities.

As a teenager, you are cast in many different roles. You may be a son or daughter, a friend, a student, a brother or sister, a teammate, a club member, a member of a religious organization. Each of these roles is good and is something that makes certain demands on you. Each brings its own challenges and rewards.

When it comes to understanding your true self, however, it's easy to get *what* you are confused with *who* you are. Each role exists because of circumstances in your life, and because life changes, these roles will also change. Some will disappear as others take their place. You will not be a student forever, but you may be an employee, a marriage partner, and possibly a parent. If you define and understand yourself only in terms of the roles in your life, there will be little room left for your own security and sense of yourself. Then the really beautiful aspects of your personality may go unnoticed.

Understanding yourself means going beyond the exteriors and the different roles you fill. Until you know *who* you really are, *what* you are can become frustrating and confusing.

A Self-Inventory

Check the characteristics you feel best describe you.

_____ Shy	_____ Good listener
_____ Leader	_____ Take charge

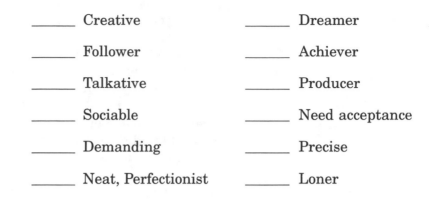

_____ Creative   _____ Dreamer

_____ Follower   _____ Achiever

_____ Talkative   _____ Producer

_____ Sociable   _____ Need acceptance

_____ Demanding   _____ Precise

_____ Neat, Perfectionist   _____ Loner

Which adjectives did you choose? Select one, and give an example of a time when your behavior illustrated that characteristic. (Example: If you described yourself as shy, recall a time when you wanted to give an answer in class or introduce yourself to someone at a party, but you didn't speak up.) Write your answer below:

Characteristic:

_____

Example:

_____

_____

Don't Worship Images

Similar to the concept of role is the concept of image. In every school students are categorized by some image they project. They may be in an accelerated class, in a special activity, or dress a certain way. Because of this, there is great danger of living up to one's image, rather than one's true identity. High school is a time when the mature adult you are becoming is definitely being formed. Understanding yourself as opposed to various "images" of you is a critical thing to learn.

People tend to like things neat and simple. As a result, it's easy to put each person we meet into some kind of pigeonhole, a neat category. Steve is an athlete. Debbie will probably be a dropout. Mike is class president. This system is simple, but is it healthy? Never!

Everyone longs for acceptance and appreciation from others. Your friends help meet those needs. And, as the months go by, you are probably getting at least enough positive response from others to make life bearable. Part of that popularity, however, may stem from an image that you have managed to establish. The problem is, you may begin to see that image of yourself as the real you. This can be seen quite often when young people get into gangs, where certain behavior and certain attitudes, as well as actions, are expected. There is usually very little creativity or self-expression in gangs, simply because the gang demands a regulated style of thought and action. Gangs are not good not only because they tend to stray outside the law; they are also some of the worst culprits in not allowing young people to grow into the mature, responsible adults they can be.

No one has much respect for the teachers who are so caught up with their image as the boss that they forget to be human. It's easy to see they have a problem. But then, it's always easy to see other people's problems. Identifying these same characteristics in ourselves, however, may take a bit more work.

Since no one likes living up to an image all the time, one solution is to start respecting others' individuality. Sure, they may belong to a particular group, and have certain kinds of friends, but beginning to take people for what they honestly are is a way of beginning to see yourself more honestly, too. No matter how great someone's image may be, it is only a hollow shell, a false front. There are no great images. There are only great people—and there is nothing to keep you from becoming one of them.

Your lifestyle and your present job as a student are part of your life. What you do for entertainment, how you see the need to be popular, the possible need to include drugs or alcohol as an essential part of entertainment, and the way you choose to look and dress are aspects of your life. But they are not the real you.

By getting caught up in what we think the world expects of us, and giving in to the pressures we feel, we may give a very distinct impression on the outside. Where it really counts, however, there may be nothing but disaster. Living in a mold we or someone else has created may make life easier for a while, but it is usually a mistake in the long run. All it does is make us moldy!

Rapping It Up

What are you really all about, anyway? For starters, as a teenager you are a person between childhood and adulthood. You are dynamic because of your thirst for a fuller life, because your goals are high and your potential is great. You are a person on the move, a changer, an innovator. You haven't gotten into the habit of settling for second best, and you know things can be better.

By understanding that you, too, are on your way to becoming better, you can build a real respect and honest appreciation of your own worth. By looking at your responses and decisions, you can evaluate your life as it is. By looking at your ability for success and your distaste for failure, you can realize the possibilities you can achieve.

Be calm and comfortable with yourself. Understand that you, as a unique individual, are more than a number in a computer in the high school office. You are special. No image or mold could possibly contain all you really are. By facing what and who you are already, you can set yourself well on the way to a fuller and richer life. Only you will set the limits you decide to accept.

Be good to yourself, and learn to smile at the mirror once in a while. The person you see there is your best friend, not your enemy. When you really like him or her, nothing can stop you.

Points to Ponder

1. List the three most important things in your life. Why are they so special to you?

_____

_____

2. Name one decision you made recently. What does it tell about your values?

_____

_____

3. How does people's image of you differ from what you really are?

_____

_____

4. Think back to one of your recent failures. What do you think was the major cause of this setback?

_____

_____

What Is High School All About?

3

While it may be normal to say you hate school as much as you like spring break, there remains another reality. Many teens learn to really enjoy their high school years.

A Fact of Life

School is a very basic fact of your life right now, and once you get beyond the stage of living up to images and stereo-types, school can become a place where you can really enjoy yourself. One of the basic principles for enjoying anything is first to understand it, recognize its value, and then learn how to cope with any problems it may bring.

Basically, the purpose of high school is to provide you with the opportunity to learn and develop to your maximum potential. Academics are important, but they are only the beginning of what high school can offer. You need to know basic facts and how to keep learning all your life in this fast-changing world. That's a fact: You need to learn. But you may win every science award available and still be miserable if you don't know how to live fully and comfortably with yourself and others. If you gain all the knowledge and skill necessary to be a computer programmer and cannot deal with fellow workers, you won't get very far! So participating in classes and passing tests are not enough to make your high school years a success or to prepare you for the future. Let's take a look at some of the skills that are also essential to this process of learning.

A, B, C, Plus You and Me

The academic subjects—English, social studies, math, and all the rest—are not really instruments of torture. Educators often assess what they teach to keep the material relevant and up-to-date. And once they decide certain forms of knowledge and skills are needed for success in society, they have an obligation to help you learn them. As the world shrinks and more competition comes from graduates all over the globe in the new century, schools must keep grade requirements high and stress mastery of essential skills.

We will be talking more about teachers later, but let's just say for now that no good teacher will challenge you unrealistically and defy you to pass his or her class. Real education is not a battle of wits, where the teachers are the bad guys, trying to outsmart the good guys, who, naturally, are the students. True learning should be the goal of any good school system, and when teachers fail to present material in a meaningful way, it is the school's fault, not the student's.

The word *education* comes from the Latin word *educare*. This word does not mean pouring facts into a person's head. It means "pulling or drawing out." Real education, then, is not pouring facts into your brain. It is drawing out all the talent and potential that is in you. Presenting the required knowledge is the job of the school. Learning as much as is individually possible is the duty of each student.

Some subjects may not seem useful to you. English may not seem important now, but when the time comes to write to that terrific person you met last summer, or you have a job interview the next day, you may wish you had paid more attention to the finer points of the language.

Math can be a drag at times, but when your checkbook balances, and you can compute financial dealings such as taxes and profit, math will become not only an ally, but a source of real pleasure.

Skills Are as Important as Subjects

What many teens fail to realize during their education is that the skills they use during school are as important as the material covered in tests. Not everyone is going to remember all the facts and bits of knowledge teachers put in exams. But skills—such as learning how to study and how to plan—will never be forgotten.

Learning how to use the library, the Internet, and react intelligently to newspapers, magazines, television, and information on the Web may not seem important when you are learning these things. When you are out of school, though, and all your knowledge must come from the media, the Internet, and other sources, those weeks of tearing apart commentators' opinions and rummaging through the school library will begin to pay off.

People 101

There is no class called "People 101." Yet one of the most valuable forms of knowledge a high school can offer is just that—learning about people.

The step from a small elementary or junior high school into a large high school is, for some, traumatic. There are so many people, so many strange faces, and so many different things people are doing! But that exposure to all kinds of people and all kinds of opinions and lifestyles can teach you some of the most important lessons you learn.

Dealing with people isn't always easy. Some will demand more than you are ready to give. Some will ridicule you for your beliefs and the ways you respond to life. Some may question your right to get in the way of their ideas. But by looking honestly at the members of your classes and those in your life right now, and then deciding what you do and don't like about them, you can begin to get a broader idea of the kind of people you will meet in the years after school. You can learn to choose your friends and deal with others on your own terms.

Watching how other teens deal with their problems can also be a big lesson. There are more teens turning to drugs and drinking now than ever before. Statistics say it is the biggest problem for teenagers and young adults right now. While you may not consider yourself a "druggie" or an addictive drinker, you may be slipping into that group. Addiction of any kind is the answer only for misery and some tough battles ahead in your life. Look at friends who are drunks or addicts, or visit the local cemetery where victims of drug and drinking abuse are buried. Then make your own decisions.

You can also learn a lot of positive things from fellow students. A former student once said he was trying to tell a certain girl how he felt about her. His shyness and lack of confidence, however, kept him from being able to carry it off. Then a friend of his, who was a popular football and baseball player, confided he had copied a seventeenth-century love sonnet they had been studying in English. He had given the copy to his girlfriend. This football player may have had a big macho image with everyone else, but he was also his own man. He had no fear of showing his gentle side when it came to the tender things of life.

The student took his example from that friend's courage, and also copied the poem. After slipping it in the girl's notebook, he began what turned out to be a good relationship. Without the courage he gained from his friend's stronger conviction, though, that boy might still be sitting in the back of class, worrying about how to approach a girl and not believing in himself.

The Team Approach

Another value of working with people during your high school years is the experience you can get by submerging your own efforts into a group. The teen years are when most young people are trying to find their own individuality. So they can sometimes get so self-involved they forget they don't have to do everything themselves.

State championships are not usually won by all-stars. The team of players who can make the sacrifice, and give up some of their own glory once in a while for the good of the team, are the ones who win in the end. By working with others in group efforts such as plays, yearbooks, and newspapers, clubs and class projects, you can learn how to deal with different kinds of people. It will give you a good idea of what the world of work in adult life is all about, and it will help you realize you don't always have to work for things alone.

Developing both leadership and teamwork skills is as important as writing a good composition or passing math class.

Rapping It Up

School is one of the few places left in our society where what is unknown or sometimes faulty is just as important as that which is positively sure and perfectly correct. If we knew everything, every teacher alive would be out of a job! Being a student gives you the luxury of being wrong once in a while, and you don't need to feel you have failed when you don't learn something the first time. You have the luxury of going back at it and trying again.

Take advantage of these years when you are expected to learn through trial and error. Don't be afraid to discard things about yourself or your life that you feel don't fit any more.

Yours is the luxury of changing your mind and rearranging your perspective, so go ahead and do it, as long as you are convinced of the worth of your actions and the possible good that can come from them. High school is a time to pick and choose, to learn and develop all that you can, and to form patterns of living and responding that will last a lifetime.

What is high school all about? It's about you! It is about the best possible you—the person who can some day walk away from the teachers, the books, and the circumstances that make this time of your life so exciting and challenging.

School exists for you—not you for it. Remember this, and take the best high school has to offer as you count those months until graduation.

Points to Ponder

1. What is one specific thing you dislike about school?

_____

Is there anything reasonable you can do about the problem? If so, what? If not, how can you rise above it?

_____
_____
_____
_____

2. What lessons have you learned lately by watching your fellow students and seeing how they do things?

_____
_____
_____
_____

3. How have you changed since this time last year?

_____
_____
_____
_____

4. List some after-school activities that attract you. Why do these appeal to you?

_____
_____
_____
_____

Attitude | 4

One thing no one can tolerate is injustice. Suppose one student gets caught smoking marijuana and is suspended for the entire semester. Another is also nabbed, but is suspended for only three days, then returns to school with all credits and privileges intact.

"Unfair!"

The cry of injustice can be heard from the gym to the cafeteria, and teens shake their heads and point to the rotten state of fair play and equal treatment in their school.

These situations do occur, and there is a logical explanation for them. There may have been different circumstances surrounding the two cases, and there also may have been very different attitudes on the part of the offenders. Many decisions made by administrators and those in authority are influenced by that slippery, intangible thing called attitude. Some people can make the best of bad situations because of their attitude, while others may get hurt by their own words because they respond to difficulty by creating more difficulty.

Attitude is really a response. It is the way you deal with life, and comes from inside you and your personality. Attitude is the basic pattern you have for dealing with people and circumstances, and it has developed through your own heredity and the individual world in which you live. If you really like who you are and who you are becoming, you will probably be at ease with your attitude toward people and things. If you are unhappy, your attitude will probably mirror your misery. And there aren't many people out there who willingly keep misery or miserable people around them.

Accentuate the Positive

One of the surest ways of surviving, and even succeeding, in high school is beginning with a positive approach. Some teens drag themselves through the school doors every day, dreading every minute they are trapped in that academic jail, and marking off the days until vacation like prisoners awaiting release. These students are only encouraging their own misery and lack of success in school.

Any winning coach will tell you that when the team is convinced they can win, they probably will. Positive mental attitude does give you a chance at success. Students who set realistic academic goals and then believe they can reach them will probably surprise many with their success. Attitude and mental conviction are powerful things.

Every year awards are given to students and players who have shown good attitude, and bookstores and the Internet are full of material that tells you how to develop a winning attitude for any aspect of life. The trouble with attitude is that you don't see it. You don't get a grade for it, and just when you think you have it pinned down, it slips away and turns up in a way you never expected. Once controlled, however, it can make you unstoppable!

One Success Story

Attitude is a difficult thing for many people to explain. "I don't like your attitude" is as close as most adults get in discussions with teens, but they don't always tell you exactly what that means.

What adults are trying to say is what they have discovered from their successes and failures in life—that an open, positive approach to life, liking yourself and liking the challenges you meet, is the best way to be happy and successful.

A positive attitude and self-confidence can bring you success, too. For example, one student's extra weight was causing embarrassment and frustration. It was standing in the way of a happier life. Like too many teens, some of her classmates were very cruel to this student. She tried every diet and form of weight reduction, but got no results.

Then one day, the student simply decided to lose weight. With her new assumption it would work and her determination to make it happen, the weight began to come off! Her will power and ability to stick to a regimen of proper eating were phenomenal, and by the time it was over, she had lost fifty-five pounds. What emerged from this "battle of the bulge" was a new person, and one who learned she could make things happen by keeping a positive attitude. And because of the self-respect that girl developed, the respect of others followed. By proving that with the proper attitude she could attain seemingly unreachable goals, the girl emerged with an entirely new, positive outlook on life.

A positive approach to life and its many problems can make all the difference. Many young people, feeling the pressures and demands of school, begin to think the world is out to get them. There seem to be so many obstacles to success, so few rewards, and the challenges never stop coming. Because of this stress, teens can easily develop a negative attitude toward adults, authority figures, and anything that seems not to fit in their present world. Those who work on maintaining a more positive attitude, however, have a much better chance of succeeding in high school, and the rest of life afterward.

Inventory

Do you find negative attitudes in your home? In your friends? Give examples.

_____

_____

_____

What brings out a negative attitude in you? What are your negative "buttons"?

_____

_____

_____

Name a problem or difficult situation you face. List some positive things you could do to solve or improve it.

_____

_____

_____

_____

Chronic Cynicism

One of the greatest illnesses teens can pick up today is a nasty thing called Chronic Cynicism. Maybe the media encourages teens to grow up too fast, but some of our best young people have developed a defensive attitude where they begin to put down almost everything and pass judgment on anything that crosses their paths.

It may give these people a false sense of superiority, and it may be their way of fighting back against all the putdowns they have received, but Chronic Cynicism is a personality killer, and it can be very contagious.

Everyone can think of some adult they know who is bitter, narrow-minded, negative, and cynical. These people are not loved a great deal, and most people avoid them. But you need to remember these miserable people did not become that way overnight. It took years of steady training, and one negative reaction after another, to bring these people to their current state. Guess where some of them began? Right! In their high school years!

If you or any of your friends are victims of Chronic Cynicism, get a grip. Listen to some good music. Take a walk. Return a smile. Do anything that will bring the good and positive things of this world back into focus for you.

The Right Attitude Is the Right Approach

Developing the right attitude is a sure way of ensuring a successful, happy high school career, and a lifetime of more of the same. Being open first to yourself, and then to others, will make you easier to get along with. It will also make you much more approachable and able to make new friends. Negative and cynical people repel others.

A positive attitude is not unrealistic or sugary. It is possible to be aware of problems and be strong enough to initiate change when necessary, to take the hard knocks of life, and still maintain an open, positive attitude.

Rapping It Up

Remember the students who were caught smoking? Why did one get the book thrown at him while another got by with much more lenient punishment?

The student who was expelled for the entire semester had a chip on his shoulder, spoke sarcastically to all authority figures, and thereby invited adults to return his anger with harshness and the worst possible punishment. This student went into the principal's office expecting the worst, and let the principal know by his negative and surly attitude. Therefore, he got the worst!

The other student approached the principal with honest realism. He tried to be sincere, admitting his guilt and expressing regret for the action. His positive attitude toward punishment and his own failure made the administrator more humane and lenient. This student was granted a chance to see his mistakes, acknowledge them, and grow. The principal also gave this second student lesser punishment.

Your attitude should always be honest, but it should also be realistic and positive. By approaching your high school career in an open and optimistic manner, you give yourself a big advantage over others. You can build positive life skills by taking each day as it comes, expecting the best, realizing what is happening, and working for improvement.

You may not be the most intelligent person in your school, but nothing can keep you from becoming the most positive!

Points to Ponder

1. How would you rate your attitude toward school? More positive? More negative? Why?

_____

_____

_____

2. Is your attitude toward yourself more positive or negative? Why?

_____

_____

_____

3. Name one time you showed some Chronic Cynicism. Why did it happen?

_____

_____

_____

4. Can you think of any people whose sour attitude ruins their effectiveness with others? What would you say to them if you had the chance?

_____

_____

_____

The Classroom

Today's high school classroom is one of the most exciting and stimulating places you can be. There are new advances in technology, teacher certification, class offerings now available for moving into this new century, and it is you, the students of the 21st century, who are now benefiting from these advances.

With other countries from Japan to the new European powerhouses already profiting from strong educational systems, the United States is now answering with quality. Business leaders, congressional leaders, and educators are now committed to greater knowledge provided in today's classrooms, and you are the one to benefit from this renewed initiative.

Now all it will take is some concentrated initiative of your own.

Study the Schedule First

Debbie is a junior now. Last month she decided she wanted to go into nursing. A visit to her counselor and a check of her credits, however, revealed some low grades in science as well as some gaps in the requirements Debbie's school of choice demands. As a result, Debbie may have to take some classes in an adult education program or summer school, and she may not be able to enter the nursing school right after graduation. There also is a chance those low science grades may make acceptance to that nursing school questionable.

Of course, there is no way any teen can be expected to know at the time first-year schedules are being made exactly what career he or she will pursue. It is, however, possible to keep options open, and to protect your future by doing your best in the basic academic classes.

Choosing the right schedule may seem confusing for freshmen, but counselors are available. With their knowledge of what colleges and specialized schools require, they can give good advice. Many times teens never realize how much help is available, and how easy it is to plan alternative classes.

Most high schools offer elective classes in many different fields. These range from journalism and creative metal working to stagecraft and business management. Preparing for the future in this century requires a solid understanding of the basics, but it also helps to explore elective classes for possible occupations or hobbies in your adult world. Taking advantage of after-school and summer school programs of increased class offerings is also an option you should consider.

One of the best things you can do throughout your high school career is getting to know your counselor. Drop by the office from time to time. Check into what is new in requirements and credits, and see how you are progressing. Report cards may be enough to keep your parents happy every few months, but your parents aren't going to live your adult life. If you really intend to get all you can out of the academic experience, some honest talks with your counselor can open up new horizons and new possibilities for you.

Easy Street May Be a Dead End

One temptation for teens, which is often even more inviting if friends choose that path, is the opportunity to sign up for easy classes. Every high school has some classes that don't require extensive homework and are considered easy credits. If you are not aware of any of these classes in your school, you've probably not been out of your locker for the past six months.

The best way to choose classes is to look at what your interests are and where you believe you will learn the most. The world is full of adults who admit making the mistake of taking too many "easy" classes while in school. Now they regret passing up opportunities. Many now enrolled in adult education programs or stuck in low-paying, dead-end jobs look at today's high school schedules and wish things had been different for them.

Sliding by is always the easiest way to go. The only trouble with it is that you sometimes fall down! Take advantage of a balanced and challenging course of study. You'll never regret it.

Learn How You Learn Best

One of the greatest problems education still faces is trying to give all students the same opportunity to learn. With accelerated classes for advanced students, more basic classes for those who need more help, and new learning involvement techniques now operable in many schools, basic education is still very much the same.

Not all students learn best by reading and watching the teacher write on a chalkboard. Almost 50 percent of students are eye-minded. They learn by seeing, by reading, and by remembering what they have seen. The traditional educational process is still geared to them, with teachers requiring students to read textbooks, copy notes from the board, and write reports from information gained through the Internet. Eye-minded students usually do well in school because they are able to respond to this kind of teaching. They have a definite advantage. It you tend to remember where you saw an ad in a magazine, and even remember what corner of the page it was in, you are prob-ably eye-minded. You're lucky.

Ear-minded persons learn best by sound, by remembering what the teacher said. They will do better in lecture classes, and when forced to read material alone, they may lose interest and fail to remember key points.

Parents often complain that their children are bright and alert at home, know all the answers when quizzed, but then fail to do well at school. If ear-minded persons were given oral tests they would probably raise their grade averages considerably. Often, however, no one realizes why the ear-minded students are having difficulty. Soon the students begin to think they are just not very intelligent. If you have trouble with spelling or are a slow reader, you may be ear-minded. You are still a person with great potential for learning.

Students who feel they may be ear-minded should try using tape recorders for important lectures. They should try studying aloud when possible, and discuss subject matter with others. Ear-minded people make up about 40 percent of every student body.

The other 10 percent, action-minded people, are at the greatest disadvantage of all in the normal school process. Action-minded students learn best by doing, by working with their hands, and actually holding and handling, with personal experience of learning matter. The best way action-minded students can cope with school is to write notes and make outlines of important material, complete with pictures. Devising key symbols for main ideas and making diagrams and even cartoons can help impress facts on their minds. When choosing classes, action-minded people would be wise to go heavy on lab classes, where book work is only part of the program, and where it is possible to learn the most by actually doing.

The First Week

Now comes the big question. "I walk into class on the first day. What do I do? How can I really succeed?"

The first week or two of any new semester should be a time of studying and judging, and the first thing you should do is study the one thing that will determine everything else that will happen in that classroom. You study the teacher.

Your success in any subject depends heavily on how well you understand the teacher and what he or she expects from you. First take a look at that person as a human being. Does the teacher seem comfortable and at ease, or overly formal? Strict formality is a clue that he or she is very image-conscious and will probably run a very tight ship!

Is the teacher interested in getting to know the students' names, or does he or she immediately get down to business? If the teacher immediately begins teaching, he or she is probably most concerned with getting the subject matter across, and you may find yourself in an uphill battle if you want to assert your identity in that classroom.

The teachers who try to get to know their students at the beginning of a new class may turn out to be the ones you turn to with a problem or in a time of crisis. If you find the teacher encouraging discussion and trying to learn names quickly, you have just signed on with a person who is probably aware of his or her own individuality and who may encourage you to find yours. This type of teacher will also want you to give your opinions on topics that arise. In most cases, you can expect the teacher to at least be aware of you as a unique person.

Studying the personalities of your teachers will give you a good idea of what your classes will be like and help you decide how to spend your limited study time. By knowing what the instructor will expect, and what he or she feels is important, you can begin to get the class under control in your mind and relieve any pressures you may have felt going into it.

Introduce Yourself

"The last thing in the world I want is for the teacher to know me," you might say. "The farther away I can stay, the better off I'll be!"

Not true. Sooner or later your presence will become known. If nothing else, you may be absent one day, and the teacher will ask who sits there! The teacher will know who you are, all right, so that argument won't work. You might as well use that knowledge to your best advantage.

One of the best things you can do sometime during the first few weeks is to stop in before or after school and let your teacher know a little bit about yourself. For example, you may mention you like horses.

"How about that! I have one of my own," the teacher may respond.

What has happened? You and the teacher have just stopped being just a name on a class list. You have found something in common, and for the rest of your time together, your teacher will be more interested in you and your progress—or lack of it—just because he or she knows you a little better.

If stopping by to see a teacher is too much to ask from you right now, at least begin by greeting the teacher before class. There are times when high schools must look like monasteries, because the students file into the room, never looking at the teacher, and never even saying, "Hi."

Students can also pass a teacher in the hall and stare right past him or her, as if the teacher were part of the woodwork. Acknowledging someone who is spending the better part of an hour with you five days a week is just a decent and polite thing to do. It can be one more way for you to let that teacher know you as an individual. It can also be one more way for you to let that teacher know you *are* an individual. That's the beginning of success in the classroom.

Another reason for making yourself known to any instructor is to explain any problems you have. Telling teachers about problems you have in their class, or simply letting them know you fear failure in their subject, is not polishing the apple. It is just one way you can protect yourself from a lack of understanding. And sometimes just telling someone about your problems gets them into the open and under control.

There are two parts of a very special concept called learning. The teacher cannot succeed without you—and you cannot succeed without the teacher. Teach the teacher about yourself. If he or she doesn't know you, you will never have all the help you could have had in a particular class.

Let the Teacher Teach

Now comes the process that your parents are paying taxes or tuition for, and that is the biggest job in your life right now. You learn! Or at least you try!

Handling each class is like handling any situation in life. Just as you read in Chapter 3, the goal of education is to prepare you for the future and give you the experience you'll need to meet life head on.

Leaning is simply a process of adding new knowledge to things that are already a part of you. It is a building process. Although daily progress may be hard to see, the structure does eventually appear.

Each class has its own unique style, because each class has its own unique teacher. And even the same teacher does not teach two classes exactly the same way each year, because the students are different. One group may ask more questions, so the teacher will respond to that. Another group may be harder to handle because one or two students create discipline problems. This need for discipline will make the teacher stick to the strict lesson plan. Some classes are very quiet because students are afraid of ridicule from others. In these cases, the teacher will be more formal.

The best class you can have is one in which students feel free to ask questions. You are a part of it, and part of your job is participation. Don't be afraid to look puzzled or raise a hand once in a while. What you don't know can be important. If you don't understand a particular concept, you can be sure someone else doesn't understand it either. By asking questions, you can help others learn. Sitting passively through class day after day only makes you bored and gives the teacher the idea that you don't care.

Inventory

What kind of student are you? Check the items that you think apply to you.

_____ Non-caring

_____ Under pressure from parents for grades

_____ Grade-conscious

_____ Bored

_____ Hardworking

_____ Self-motivated

_____ Afraid of failure

_____ Pressured by classmates not to excel

_____ The ideal student

_____ No desire to succeed in school

_____ A nonreader

_____ Other problems take priority over school

_____ No time for homework

_____ Not interested in much

Now that you've checked this list, find the negative items on it. They will be the things that keep you from success in the classroom. You can face these problems and possibly share them with your teacher. They are your first homework. Thinking through ways to bring these problems down to size is the first step toward solving them.

Learn to Spot What Is Important

Any class will contain a lot of material. If you are really aware of the teacher, you can spot the information that he or she is trying to stress. What teachers repeat often, they want you to learn. What they write on the board should go in your notes. Some of the course material will be background and is not essential. You must learn to spot key points. Some stores have a flashing blue or red light to call attention to special values. Learn to spot the signals that your teacher is hitting the important facts.

What does the teacher review at the beginning of class? What does he or she refer back to in examples? How intense is the teacher when talking about a certain thing? What does he or she write on the board? All these are clues that separate the meat from the fluff in any class, and they should give you a better idea of what is important.

Learning to listen also helps. Teens are good at looking directly at the teacher while their minds are far away, thinking about the latest concert or that new boutique in the mall. True, there will be times when your mind wanders, but try to keep it in tow most of the time. Some students get so involved watching a teacher's idiosyncrasies or noticing he needs a haircut that they lose track of what the teacher is saying. Get all your noticing out of the way at the beginning of class. Then settle down, and try to give the teacher your full attention.

The Great Homework Conspiracy

Most classes come with an extra, added attraction: homework! This word can strike terror into the heart of any freedom-loving high schooler, but it is something we cannot pass by. A word first about the great homework conspiracy.

In any high school, usually in the morning before classes begin, there will be students sitting in the halls, on the school bus, or in an empty classroom madly copying someone else's homework. Some students work out elaborate plans for beating homework assignments, with each individual responsible for part of the load. These students meet at a given place, exchange work, and then rush off to class, thinking they have fooled the teachers and beaten the system.

Not quite. Any alert teacher knows what is going on. And while new studies often criticize some schools for giving too much homework, the concept of homework in high school has now been refined to a study of needed skills and knowledge. Because adult life demands that people gain new knowledge by reading or using the media, homework attempts to teach this skill along with the subject matter itself.

Homework Hints

The secret to handling the homework problem lies in understanding assignments for what they really are. Some work, such as reading, involves real learning. It is necessary for keeping up with the class, and learning to keep up in high school will make college much easier. Other assignments are drills. Once you know the material, you can complete the work quickly and reinforce what you've learned at the same time.

Take a tip from college students. Many ask a teacher at the beginning of a semester to outline the class and discuss assignments, projects, and expectations. In that way students get an overview of the class and can plan their schedules accordingly.

A teacher will be glad to tell you what a class is all about. Your question is a chance for the teacher to show that he or she is organized and in control.

Knowing what a class involves will also give you time to plan for the end-of-semester blitz, when every teacher seems to assign long projects, and you are faced with the task of completing them as well as studying for finals. By getting some of the work out of the way early, you can keep your sanity before report card time. You can also give yourself the advantage of enjoying life while your friends are burning the candle at both ends as the semester draws to a close.

Let's get specific. How can you sensibly tackle homework?

When homework is given, assess how much concentration and time are required. Some work can be handled while you are baby-sitting. Other material will need your best attention—a quiet place and as much mental strength as you are able to muster. But be careful that you don't reach the point where you feel you cannot concentrate without absolute silence and privacy. If you feel you can only do decent thinking under such perfect conditions, you will be setting up an unreal situation. Absolute silence and privacy are rare, so learn to tune out distractions. The ability to concentrate even with distractions around you will be an asset for the rest of your life. Today's world demands the ability to concentrate in all kinds of situations. Learn now to shut the world out and zero in on what you're doing. It will make success easier all through your life. It will also keep you from becoming an impossible person on any team that needs to get a job done.

Long-term projects are another matter. They require research and involve hours of outside effort. Doing papers may be frightening at first, but once you learn how to plan for them and pace yourself in the time allotted, you can handle them.

If you plan on going to college, you are learning a valuable lesson if you can do these papers with a minimum of tension and time. You will also be far ahead of others who have never had to discipline themselves to this degree. Using a combination of Internet material and library and personal research, you can learn to pace yourself. Developing a plan of attack for long projects, with a time schedule as a guide, can help you learn to handle big projects with ease. That's a lesson that will serve you the rest of your life.

Give It Your Best Effort

The best teacher in the world and the most expensive computers are of no use if you do not begin to assimilate the material that is presented. No one can give you learning, just as no one can give you a fine athletic body or musical ability.

Learning is work—pure and simple. It is also one of the most rewarding aspects of life on the planet.

Studying is not easy. It is something you must do by yourself, and it is one of the things that will take your greatest effort. It is easy to ride along and squeak by on tests, stay on the surface of the subject matter, and promise that tomorrow you will really begin to learn. The longer you wait, however, the more you'll miss. And the less you'll have going for you when you step out into the "real world." A good way to begin studying is to set tangible goals. An A may be unrealistic for you, so it is good to use something other than grades as your standard. A realistic goal may be the ability to tell someone else, even if it's your kid brother, what you've learned. If you can teach it to someone else, you really know it!

Give study time your best effort, set some realistic goals, and reward yourself when you are finished. The amount of time you spend studying is not as important as the quality of that time. If you can give yourself to some honest work for an hour, do it.

Learn to concentrate, which means giving your attention to one particular thing. It is never easy, but unless you develop the ability to do it during your teen years, you may never again have the opportunity to master this skill.

Find a place with some semblance of peace where you will be comfortable. If music in the background helps you relax, use it. However, trying to really concentrate with the top hits blaring through your headphones is not the answer. The adult world has learned to use music as background at times, and as entertainment at others. When you want to listen to your favorite tunes, give them the attention they deserve. When the time is set aside for study, leave the headphones on low or off.

If you need a break once in a while, take it. Walk around. Watch a bit of TV or scan the Web a bit. Raid the refrigerator if your conscience allows it. Then come back, put everything else on the side, and get to work again.

Reward yourself when your goals are reached. Go ahead and give yourself a treat when you've given your best to something. Let yourself feel success, and don't be afraid to be proud of your achievements. Study is hard work, and if you have done it well, you should be proud.

Someone once remarked to the author James Thurber, "You must love to write because you write so much."

Thurber surprised that person by answering, "I hate writing. But I love having written."

That sums how most people feel about studying. It's never easy, but you will love having learned and accomplished the goals you set for yourself.

What you learn is not for the teacher, your folks, or your friends. The information you learn in high school will be part of you forever. If you are smart enough to take the best of what it has to offer, you're smarter than some people may think you are, and you are a richer person as well.

Rapping It Up

The term "classroom" has many meanings to many people. When we talk about having class or being classy we are describing something, or someone, of high quality. It is interesting, then, that we should call that place where learning takes place a *class* room. In a way, class comes from knowing what and who you are. If learning is taking place, that time you spend sitting behind a desk or computer could be time for picking up some real class.

Success in school is your challenge and your job right now. If you take time to pick your classes wisely with an eye to the future, get to know yourself and your teachers, and give the material they present your honest best, you will succeed. You will not only be a good student, but a real winner.

If you do your best in the classroom, you certainly can become a very classy person!

Points to Ponder

1. Think back about why you chose the elective classes you did. What were your reasons?

_____

_____

_____

2. Which study method works best for you? Are you eye-minded, ear-minded, or action-minded?

_____

_____

_____

3. What is the hardest subject for you to learn?

_____

What is your main problem in studying this subject?

_____

Have you told your teacher about this problem? Have you told anyone?

_____

4. How could you get your teachers to know you more as a person?

_____

_____

Making the Grade 6

Society likes success. It seems everyone demands to see tangible proof that something has gone well. The successful businessperson buys a fancy car and moves to a higher-class neighborhood. The superstar makes a big splash with a phenomenal wardrobe and dazzling jewelry. The doctor hangs his or her medical diploma on the wall.

In high school there is also a way of showing a measure of success in work. It's called—a report card!

How Did I Do?

It is natural to want to know how well we are doing. In the work world, we get this feedback from reviews and possible raises in salary. In school, we call that process grading.

The problem with grades comes from the great importance they carry. If Dave's report card is all right, Mom and Dad may be satisfied. The actual learning of subject matter and the real mastery of skills can somehow fall by the roadside.

One of the greatest things you can do for yourself is not work for grades for anyone else's satisfaction. The real test will be: are *you* satisfied?

You should also develop a more realistic attitude toward the grades that finally show up on your report card. They are important; they indicate how well you have passed the tests, done the work, and mastered what the teacher determines is essential material. But the real objective is learning, not passing. The world is full of adults who have survived high school, in the sense that they passed their classes and walked out with a diploma. But they have not graduated with the mastery and knowledge they could have attained, and they are often unhappy with themselves because of it.

Settling for a passing grade may make your life easier now, but it also gets you into a dangerous attitude in which you are content with mediocrity. There are times all through life when one can say with satisfaction, "This will do." But if we begin to lower our standards with important things, we may dig some deep ruts that can only damage our work ethic and chances for success in years to come.

Work Ethic: What Is It?

Recently a supervisor of a top insurance company confided, "I have to fire fifteen people next week. They're all under twenty-eight, and I hate to do it. But they have no commitment to the company. They put in their time, and leave right at the end of the day. All they care about is getting a good paycheck with great benefits, but not about helping the company survive."

Sad? Yes. Why did it happen?

The answer is a concept called *work ethic*. It doesn't show up directly on a paycheck, but in the work world, it is one of the most important thing bosses and top administrators look for.

A strong work ethic can lead to success in high school and in later life. It is reflected in your attitude toward the work at hand, and it conveys itself to your employers and coworkers. Work ethic determines how seriously you give yourself to a project, how much motivation goes into any piece of work. It separates the winners from the also-rans. The athlete with talent doesn't always make it to the pros. If an athlete doesn't have a strong work ethic that drives him or her to stay physically in top shape, learn game plans, and always strive to win, he or she will fail.

Check the following statements that apply to you:

_____ My pleasure is very important	_____ I am goal-oriented
_____ I need to be part of the group	_____ I can work alone
_____ I have a right to a good job	_____ I earn the things I get
_____ I have to please my folks	_____ I enjoy my own success
_____ Short-term projects are best	_____ I can see any project through
_____ I am profit-motivated	_____ I am self-motivated
_____ More work is a bore	_____ I can enjoy the product of work
_____ I'm not really a winner	_____ I believe in my ability to work
_____ I work when I have to	_____ Sometimes work is enjoyable

If you put the most checks in the left column, your work ethic is poor. Your own pleasure is still more important than your success. You have some hard growing up to do.

If you put the most checks in the right column, your work ethic is on track. Now your task is not to be better than others, but rather to be better than yourself as you are now.

Where Did This Grade Come From?

A good question. And the answers to it are important, because they help you understand the grades you will see on your next report card.

The first thing to understand is that each class has a rating and evaluation system of its own. When your teacher gives you a math grade, it comes from a series of test scores and homework assignments. How many problems did you get right? How much work did you accomplish? In a math class, the grading system is simple and always objective. It doesn't matter if you smiled at the teacher, spent hours studying, or breezed through the class because it was easy. The grade simply shows how many answers you got right or wrong.

Any class in which your grade is determined in an objective manner is one in which you can keep track of progress yourself. By keeping your test scores, you can know what your average is, and you can do something about it before the grading period ends.

This Subject Is Too Subjective!

In other classes, where the grading is more subjective, your progress can be harder to assess. How well you complete a project in shop or a home economics class is something the teacher determines. The grade does not reflect right or wrong answers but comes from meeting a defined set of standards that the teacher uses to evaluate your work.

When you hand in an English composition, there may be points off for misspelling or grammatical errors. Even though English teachers often use two grades—one for content and one for technical skills—the grade tends to be subjective. In classes such as these, it is wise to talk to the teacher from time to time and ask what he or she expects. If you can understand the teacher's standards, you have a better chance of meeting them when grade time nears.

Too many students go blindly ahead on projects, do what *they* feel is right, and then hand them in. When they get the grade, they complain, then develop negative and bitter feelings. Once that grade is given, though, it is too late. Knowing *beforehand* is the only way to set your own standards and understand what is expected of you.

One thing you will want to check is that your grade comes only from your academic progress. A good reporting system may include grades given for conduct and effort, but they should be separate from academic grades.

If you have a tendency to talk a lot in class, or for some reason make the teacher feel you are a discipline problem, this should not be reflected in your academic grade. Your may get an A in the subject and an F in conduct, but these grades should be separate. If you feel there is some problem in this area, talk to the teacher to try to set things straight.

Changing Grades

Teachers dread report card day as much as students, but what they really dislike is knowing some students will invariably come after report cards have been handed out, asking or demanding that a grade be changed.

The time for worrying about grades is during the grading period. Once that time is over and a teacher has come up with averages and grades, he or she is not terribly excited about being challenged on a particular mark. Don't let yourself become one of the angry horde that moves from classroom to classroom after school on report card day, arguing and pleading with teachers to change grades.

However, if you feel a grade is unjust or a mistake has been made, you have every right to approach a teacher. Just be prepared to do it in a reasonable manner. Carrying on and moaning that you will be grounded or lose your car privileges is not a mature or acceptable way of behaving. It only lowers the teacher's opinion of you and marks you as a whiner who has probably gotten by for years with similar tactics. It is also bad for your own self-esteem. If classmates see you go into your routine, they may not have much respect for you, either!

Safe at Home?

Report cards are meant for your parents as well as for you. The school wants to communicate your progress to the home front, and report cards are so far the best way to do that. This is especially necessary in high school, when most parents do not meet or communicate on a regular basis with their children's teachers.

One way you can soften the blow of report cards is to encourage your parents to meet teachers during open house or parent meetings. Personal communication is more satisfactory than a cold grade plunked on a computer-printed card. It will also give both your folks and your teachers a better understanding of each other, as well as you.

Some parents, sad to say, put unreal pressure on their children. If Dad was a Rhodes Scholar and all your older brothers and sisters came home with straight A's, you may be under the gun to bring home nothing less. If you feel your parents expect more than you can honestly deliver, an attempt at communication will go a long way. Your parents want you to be a success, and they want you to be the best you can be. That's normal. If you feel they don't understand some of your problems in a particular class, however, it is up to you to get that message across in a calm way.

Unfair Grades

You may also run into a class where a teacher is a hard grader, and an A is difficult to come by. You may meet a male teacher who feels it is impossible for a girl to get an A in Driver's Ed, or a teacher who thinks a master computer would have difficulty pulling a top grade in her calculus class.

Such teachers are rare, but they do exist. If you happen to get them for a class during your school career, you may have to learn another lesson early in life. If you feel the teacher is difficult, let your parents know about the situation in advance. This will help make the report card go down a bit easier. If, however, you feel you are the victim of real discrimination—be it because of your sex, race, or any other minority status—you do have avenues for seeking help. First of all, follow the chain of command. This is the proper way to handle any problem—now and in the future.

The first person you address is the teacher. Express your concerns, and ask for some straight answers. If the situation does not change, your next step is the department head. Is an English teacher your problem? Ask for a meeting with the English department head and express your concerns. If no help is given, go to the principal. State and federal laws are very definite on discrimination, and your principal is very aware of them.

You may be young, but you do have the right to fair and unbiased treatment. Don't be afraid to claim that right.

Reading a Report Card

Reports cards are not just for your parents: they are for you, too. If you take them and just slip them into your pocket until that fateful moment at home, you're missing something you can do for yourself.

Fearing report cards can rob you of a valuable source of information. Any coach who loses a game tries to understand why. He or she takes an honest look at where things could have gone better. The coach then makes corrections and comes out fresh for the next game. If a coach dwelled on past failures, he or she would never have the courage to go out and try again.

In the same way, you can learn to make report cards work for you and guide you to a more successful school experience. Let them be a tool, not a torment. Use them well, and then move on to the next grading period.

Points to Ponder

1. Do you get your biggest pressure for grades from your parents or yourself?

_____

2. Are grades becoming more important or less important to you?

_____

Why?

_____

_____

3. Are you achieving realistically high standards? Explain.

_____

_____

_____

4. How can you use your report card to help understand your own success or lack of it?

_____

_____

_____

5. Grade your work ethic. _____. Now, write a short paragraph on how your attitude and approach to work and projects could be improved. List specific things you could do to improve the quality of your schoolwork and get better grades.

_____

_____

_____

_____

_____

_____

_____

_____

_____

_____

_____

_____

_____

_____

Teachers and Administrators

7

That old joke, "It's not the school, it's the principal of the thing" still gets a laugh, but many teens see no humor in the presence of teachers and administrators in their schools. Teachers have always been the object of jokes and scathing humor. They stand in front of the classroom as the adults in charge; they make the decisions, and some of them have earned the true dislike of their students. Teachers, however, are also human, and some of them can claim partial responsibility for the success of thousands of students and former students.

As teens begin to find more independence within and outside of the home, they are justified in their attempts to prove themselves. In school, however, something happens. Just when parents have begun to allow more freedom, a new set of authority figures comes in and takes over. Teachers, counselors, hall monitors, the principal, and assistant principals appear on the scene armed with rules, regulations, and student handbooks. No wonder teens, especially if they have trouble coping with authority figures, soon develop a negative attitude toward adults in the school.

Not All Teachers Are Terrific

Before you decide how you feel about teachers, remember that it's best not to think of them as a group, just as you shouldn't think of members of a profession, race, or other identity group as all being the same. Of course, you and everyone else can tell stories about bad teachers who ridicule their students, who make unreasonable demands, and who may have caused serious psychological harm to young people. These, fortunately, are a small minority.

Any teacher who is a problem to others is in exactly the same position as a problem student. It is not normal to be bitter, cynical, or lack respect for others. When people possess these characteristics, no matter what their age, they have problems. Some teachers cannot tolerate their opinion being challenged, and view open discussion as a threat to their authority. The biggest lesson these instructors can teach you is a very important one—don't be like them.

Are There Any Good Teachers?

Once you can get beyond your own hangups about authority, you may begin to realize that many teachers have a lot to offer. A good teacher who is enthusiastic about his subject matter can spur you on to new interests. He or she can challenge you to reach down and find talent and ability inside yourself that you may never have known existed. A good teacher can also become a guide who understands and really wishes the best for you.

The teacher who tries to see you as an individual and who is aware of your needs and problems can help in many ways. He or she may sometimes give you help or advice on matters that go beyond the classroom.

Student Attitude Versus Teacher Attitude

If you as a student walk into class with a chip on your shoulder, expecting the worst, you will transmit that feeling to the teacher. And you may get the worst!

If, on the other hand, you enter each class presuming real learning and sharing can take place, most teachers will respond to that feeling and try to do their best for you. Just as your mother may get upset and never feel like cooking again if no one eats her gourmet meal, a teacher who feels no one is interested or cares may lose enthusiasm and let the class become a boring routine. Turn back to Chapter 4 and find the positive, open attitude that is possible for you. Dust it off and take it into the classroom. You may see a change in the attitude of your teachers as well.

Make Them Teach

You should expect good, honest teaching when you walk into a classroom. Teachers are now required to pass exhaustive tests to prove they both know their subject matter as well as know how to teach it. Good teachers can cover the material and keep the class interesting. Some teachers, however, may fall into a routine and present the material as they have in the past. If a topic is glossed over too lightly and you still don't understand it, raise your hand. Ask for more information. Give the teacher a chance to discuss the matter more thoroughly, and make the teacher teach. You may get a lot more than you bargained for, and you may discover that your teacher is coming to class a bit more prepared in the future.

Another way you can help yourself and the teacher is to ask him or her to relate the subject matter to your current life. A good teacher should be a master of the material, but sometimes may be too intent on covering facts, forgetting to tie those facts into the needs of your own life and future dreams. If you think a class is becoming dull, try to ask some questions that bring in current events. By bringing new material to the course, you may give your teacher a new lease on teaching, and you'll have one less boring class to worry about!

The Most Misunderstood Boss

The principal! there he or she is—innocently walking down the hall. As the principal passes, you may wonder where the ax is about to fall.

Possibly the most feared and misunderstood person in any school is the principal. Principals are at a disadvantage because they can't get to know students the way teachers can. A principal can't meet with the same individuals every day, but he or she is expected to handle countless problems, be a friend and counselor to all, and keep the entire school running on an even keel.

You may say, "Why should I care?" Well, by being in a position of authority, the principal can toss you out of school—or be a big help to you. If the principal knows you, he or she can help you with references and good advice when you choose a college or set out to find a serious job. You can be sure many businesspeople in your area know your principal. They will probably be more than willing to listen when he or she speaks. So if you can get the principal to speak well about you, you'll have a great advantage.

Try to make yourself known to the principal in some positive way during the year. A smile and a "hi" will usually do the trick. Most principals only see the small percentage of students who get into serious trouble. They are eager to meet the rest of the student body. They have a teaching background, and often miss the personal contact with students that teachers enjoy every day. By offering a friendly smile, or finding some positive way for the principal to become aware of you, you can create a powerful ally.

Help Your Own Cause

By learning to be friendly with teachers and administrators, you can make your years in school happier and more successful. You will also give yourself some good practice in dealing with authority figures. Then when you are in the adult work world, you'll have an advantage over other employees who feared the mistrusted authority during their school years and continue to do so.

Those in positions higher than yours are not necessarily tyrannical, mean, or awesome. They are simply people doing a job, and when authority figures can feel the support and positive attitude of others, they tend to be more human and understanding.

The fear and lack of trust many adults have for people in positions of authority—from police officers to politicians—did not happen overnight. Many people who carry these feelings began by fearing and mistrusting their teachers and principals. They may have had domineering parents or been abused by people who used their power in the wrong ways. Whatever their reason, those who fear authority are at a great disadvantage in life. Don't let this happen to you.

Rapping It Up

If you can learn to deal in a positive way with the people who have authority in your life, your relationships with bosses and teachers are sure to be better. You may also learn to retain your own humanity and willingness to understand when you are placed in a position of authority yourself.

Teachers and administrators are human. They will have their up and down days. They have moods, good and bad days, and moments of genius just as you do. You as a student are probably very conscious of your own individuality. You want people to respond to it. You want them to be fair and try to understand your needs. You just want some respect! Your teachers are in the same situation. Most of them are conscious of their responsibility to prepare you for the world, and most want to give you the best they can offer.

The few who are poor teachers or difficult personalities are probably out of touch with the important things in life. You will find people like them everywhere, and you must learn how to deal with them. By accepting their shortcomings and trying to understand these teachers, you can make yourself a more tolerant and humane person. You can also develop the strong advantage of being able to deal with all kinds of people, even the difficult ones.

The next time you are baby-sitting, or find yourself in some circumstance where you possess authority, take a moment to realize what is happening. How are you handling the power? You will realize that authority carries as much responsibility as it does prestige. The one who wields power has to try harder to be patient, understanding, and tolerant of others.

Most teachers know these feelings and are trying to do their best. By giving teachers your respect and consideration, you can help them accomplish their job, which is helping you learn as much as you can. With your help, teachers and administrators can give you the best they have to offer. And they can help you become your very best!

Points to Ponder

1. Name four characteristics of a good teacher.

_____

_____

_____

_____

2. How can you help your teachers have better classes?

_____

_____

_____

3. What characteristics do you dislike in some of your teachers?

_____

_____

Have you ever shown the same characteristics?

_____

What would help you get along better with teachers you dislike?

_____

_____

4. What is your attitude toward the principal and his or her assistants?

_____

Is it based on fear or real knowledge? Explain.

_____

_____

5. Would you be a good teacher or principal? Why or why not?

_____

_____

_____

Beyond the Classroom

8

Many high school graduates agree on one thing. They may have learned a good deal about traditional subjects, but of the many things they remember, most were never reflected on a report card.

Any student who walks away from high school without participating in extracurricular activities, who never sits in the stands and cheers for the home team or gets involved in the great variety of school activities, has passed up some of the happiest times and opportunities for growth he or she may see for some time. It is a mistake to think of school only as a place to put in class time and get out as quickly as possible.

As your teen years roll by, you are growing and developing. Involvement in school activities can open new avenues of interest for you and help you develop a lot of characteristics you will need as an adult. Some of the most important aspects of adult life are knowing how to give, how to accept responsibility, and how to develop and retain a sense of loyalty. As a child, you were often on the receiving end. People gave you much when you were young, but it is dangerous to expect that to continue. The older you get, the more others will expect of you. That's what adulthood is all about. Involvement in school activities can make it easier to meet those expectations.

People Skills

One class that never appears on your schedule is "People 101." The social studies, math, English, and other classes are there, but where is the class where you learn to relate to others?

Once there was a student who walked away from every grading period with A's. The teachers and principal praised him, and all seemed well. But this student, with all his knowledge and good intentions, was slipping through high school without learning to deal with people. He was nice to them, but never seemed to understand them well. As a result, he soon became an object of ridicule.

Teachers couldn't understand it. The principal thought other students were just being jealous. But the other students realized the problem. This individual was simply "out of it." He was learning all the book knowledge, but he wasn't learning the simple art of common sense. He could understand textbooks and theories, but he couldn't respond in a common, ordinary way to people.

This young man is in college now. With some luck and a few new friends, he is learning to relate better to those around him. He may be a success with books, but until he learns the simple lesson of wanting to understand others, he will have disastrous relationships with coworkers and anyone else who tries to become part of his life.

Get Involved

The fact is that books can't teach you everything. Even all the searching on the Web (for too many hours, perhaps) won't do it, either. One of the most important things you can learn is how to deal with people face to face, beyond all the chat rooms in the world and beyond all the E-mail you can crowd into one day.

If you learn to really watch the people you meet and observe their reactions, that can be a good start. Start reading people's faces, especially their eyes. Learn a little bit about body language. Do people seem comfortable and at ease around you, or for some reason are they not open to you?

Another way to improve your social skills is to get involved with outside-the-classroom activities at your school. Do you like to write, or see your work actually find its way into print? Get on the school paper or yearbook staff. Do you like to work with your hands? Join an art or car club. How about sports? Terrific! If you can't make the varsity, there is always the neighborhood sandlot game or intramurals.

Whatever you choose, your school provides dozens of opportunities to get involved with people. Extracurricular groups also provide you with projects that don't involve book learning, but which can help you deal with people and find some of your true talents. By working with others and facing the demands of new situations, you can begin to develop important people skills. In this way, common sense and the ability to read people will become part of your life.

Build Some Good Memories

There may be an adult who says, "Enjoy your high school years. They're the happiest time of your life."

That statement is sad, in a way, because if a person is really developing the maximum potential for feeling, loving, succeeding, and being fulfilled, high school will not be the greatest time of your life. As an adult, a person should be able to live a deeper and richer existence and find a fuller kind of happiness than is possible for teens.

You can take many good memories from your high school years, however. That may be what some of those adults are remembering. The times when you laugh and "go bananas"—as well as the times when you feel a quiet, confident sense of success—are indeed some of the happiest and most rewarding times of life! Involvement in extracurricular activities can give you the opportunity for some of those times.

By screaming your lungs out at a game, or being involved in the game itself, by meeting the pressure of yearbook deadlines, perfecting a special piece of music or working through the excitement of a play, you can help educate yourself. These activities will be the ones you remember when your own children are in school. They may also be your fondest memories of high school.

Yes, those adults who tell you high school was the happiest time are probably remembering the thrill of taking a bow at the spring play, or the pleasure they felt when their pet idea made it through the student council.

It's Not All Pom-Poms and Praise

There may also be times when you work hard to achieve a goal but don't reach it. You may spend hours doing a mural for a school hallway only to have someone come by and make fun of it. The story in the school paper you took three nights to complete may end up in the trash can, and after all your best effort, you might still lose the big game.

"That's exactly right," you say. "So why bother getting involved? Who needs the grief?"

You do, friend, because it's not just grief. It's learning. And that's life. Do you want to feel you are becoming an adult? Do you want to walk into a room and feel you've added something besides extra weight? Part of learning common sense and deepening yourself as a person comes with facing the difficult experiences as well as the easy. By involving yourself in something that takes the best you have to offer, you can learn what it is to really try and really give.

And the setbacks and hard times only make your final success sweeter.

Rapping It Up

So, there you sit, wondering what to do. "Life is dull," you may say. "Everything is such a bore! There's nothing to do in this town!"

Maybe you're right. You may live in the deadest area in the world, one where little entertainment is available. However, there is a solution! You can make your own entertainment by getting into the action. Telling the world you are bored is simply telling the world you can't control your own life. Not a good thing to do!

Hobbies and interests can make the difference. One way to find out what you really enjoy is to explore the possibilities that exist within your own school. By getting involved, you may even start seeing some possible career opportunities. You will also learn how to deal with people in real-life situations. You'll learn how to be a good team player, and even a good leader. You'll learn how to care about an outcome, and how to cope with pressure.

You wouldn't go on a long trip without taking all the things you think you will need. Don't give less thought to that adult life up ahead. Your chance to prepare for it isn't just in the books or on the Internet. It's also in the people. Get out where the people are, and you'll walk out of high school with a real education!

Points to Ponder

1. What keeps you from getting more involved in school activities? Can it be remedied?

_____

_____

2. What was the last school function you attended, and what did you get out of it?

_____

_____

3. How did you meet the friends you now have?

_____

_____

What kind of new friends would you like to meet and why?

_____

_____

4. What do you do to fight off feelings of boredom when they hit?

_____

_____

5. What extracurricular activities at school could be of interest to you, and why?

_____

Don't Stagnate— Communicate! 9

"Now, here's one chapter I can skip," you say. "If there's one thing I can really do well, it's talk!"

Perhaps. Before you decide, though, ask yourself if you're really able to say all you want when you talk to others. Are you satisfied with the level of communication you have with your friends? Do you let the adults in your life know what's on your mind in other ways than merely complaining or arguing? In short, are you communicating what is inside of you to the people who count?

Communication is more than words. On all its different levels, it includes body language, use of speech, and the high art of listening. The ability to share our feelings and thoughts makes humans superior to other life forms. It gives us a special edge in making life richer and more rewarding. Since we are not hermits, communication is one of our greatest tools.

No One Understands Me!

Wanting to be understood is part of the human condition. You know you're a unique person, and you want others to realize that and respond to your individuality. There are ways of asserting your feelings and making your opinions known, but sometimes teens latch on to the wrong ones.

Vandalism, for example, communicates a lack of respect and mistrust of society. The teen who rips up school or public property is shouting loudly that he or she has no use for what society values. In the same way, a teen who steals is sending a message—that he or she has supposedly found a way to beat the system. Even the casual use of drugs is one way of telling the world that you aren't very good at coping or standing strong as the real individual you are.

One of the greatest problems people of all ages face is the inability to get through to others. Teens, especially, often feel they must learn to make it alone, and as a result they keep too much inside.

That's a mistake. If you want people to understand you, you must first let them know you. Your physical appearance and the way you conduct yourself may give others some hints about who you are, but not until you open up and make an honest effort to communicate can they really begin to respond.

Open Up

One of the biggest complaints from adults is, "Teens don't talk!" True, some of your teachers may feel you have no difficulties in that regard, but many adults feel they cannot communicate with young people.

Many teens, when faced with new situations, tend to drift off to the silent sidelines. All they seem to manage is one-word answers or a series of grunts, and as a result people give up trying to get through to them.

Shyness or lack of confidence can hinder your communication skills. As a teen you may feel people are passing judgment on you, but they really are not. Most people just want to find out who you are and what you're all about. If you can relax and help them know you by talking, the rest comes naturally.

You Figure It Out

Identify possible solutions in each of these cases involving communication problems:

---

1. Brian doesn't get the after-school job he wants because the store owner says Brian doesn't speak up loudly enough to deal with people.

_____

_____

2. Julie is accused of being sneaky and possibly dishonest because she doesn't look people in the eye when talking to them.

_____

_____

3. Heather won't go out with Mark because she feels he can't carry on a decent conversation with her or any of her friends.

_____

_____

Humility and Self-Esteem

The ability to communicate presumes a few things about any individual. First, you must have a certain amount of humility and respect for others' opinions. To achieve honest communication with someone, you must want to share with that person. You have to care about him or her as a person, at least at that particular moment.

The supreme egotist is too self-absorbed to really care what anyone else thinks. He or she has never realized that communication is a two-way street. Instead, the egotist believes that others are just dying to hear what the egotist has to say.

If you can bring yourself to care about others and try to develop an honest interest in what they have to offer, you will transmit this feeling to them. And they'll be more than happy to share with you. There has been a lot made of self-esteem—the lack of it and the building of it—in recent years. Self-esteem is important in effective communication, too, because honest communication demands a healthy respect for yourself. Letting the real you come out in honest verbal exchanges with others will increase your own sense of yourself as a person. And that leads to an honest sense of worth, not because someone thinks you ought to have it, but because you honestly know it's there.

"That's a laugh," you say. "I spend half my life trying to fight put-downs, and you tell me to respect myself!"

Absolutely. It is true that by the time you reach your teens you may have been thoroughly bombarded by instructions from adults and peers to keep quiet about your accomplishments. They have told you to be humble and not think too much of yourself. But what is true humility?

Truly humble people can honestly accept what they are and what they are not. If you're a good musician, it would be foolish to say you are not. By acknowledging that fact and living comfortably with it, you are humble. Humility is simply accepting the truth about yourself, both good and not so good. If you can do that, you can learn to develop honest and realistic respect for yourself.

That self-respect will be your hidden advantage when you try to share with others. It will also be a major key to your success.

Listen with Intelligence

Nodding your head occasionally is a way of letting people feel you are listening during a conversation. Making good eye contact is another. If you want to really talk to someone, don't be afraid to ask questions, ask for more information, or even disagree at times. If a person mentions something he or she presumes you know, and you don't know it, don't be afraid to say so.

"It looked like a Henway to me," someone might say.

You have no idea what a Henway is, but rather than show your possible ignorance, you nod and flash your all-knowing look. Pretending you know what you don't know certainly can backfire, as it would in this case. If you had enough self-assurance to ask what a Henway was, your conversation would have gone like this:

"What's a Henway?"

"About five pounds!"

A trick? A joke? Maybe. But it's also a little way to catch a person playing all-knowing genius when in reality he or she is not understanding you at all. Ignorance is all right. It means you simply haven't had a chance to learn something. Stupidity, of course, is another matter;

stupidity is thinking or pretending that you do know everything!

Talk with *People*

Another way to sharpen your communication skills is to talk *with* people instead of *at* them. A good speaker is always aware of his or her audience. He or she knows them, and knows how to speak to them in a way they will find comfortable.

Real communication involves being open to others' opinions and interests. If you find you have little to say, you may not know the other person well enough. As you slowly build up knowledge of others and find a common ground, you should have plenty to talk about.

Caring about others and what interests them is the key to better communication. Once you can master this, you'll be at ease in any conversation. Others, sensing your interest, will respond in a favorable, friendly way. Everyone likes to have someone around who will listen to them.

Don't Interrupt

One common criticism of young people is that they cannot listen to more than two sentences without interrupting. Whether it's a parent trying to make a point, a teacher trying to explain why your work is not up to par, or a friend simply disagreeing with your point of view, your approach should be the same. Listen while the person has his say. Then your response can be more on target.

Listening accomplishes two things. It lets the speaker feel he or she has gotten an opinion across to you. It also makes the speaker feel there can be good communication, because by listening you show you understand what real conversation is.

Listening also helps you. By listening and really hearing what another person is saying to you, you are showing some true adult behavior. You are also showing that you have the potential of being a good friend.

Don't Play Games

Much is written about the communication gap between teens and adults. Parents and teens often feel they are speaking from two different worlds. Some teens even prefer it that way. Your boss may be a middle-aged man or woman who seems impossible to talk to, and he or she, in turn, may think there is no way to get through to you.

Sometimes even your friends seem on a different planet; something comes between you. Their interests are taking them in other directions, and you just can't seem to talk to them anymore.

In order for real communication to take place, both people must be able to relax and meet on common ground. Playing games with people, and being afraid to be honest with them, is a form of insincerity. When communication seems most difficult, that's when you need to try harder to understand the other person's concerns. No communication can take place in the home, for example, if both parents and teens refuse to acknowledge where the other is coming from. If a parent and child can sit down and share a common concern with respect for each other's opinions, however, some honest and good communication can be accomplished. And something else will happen. You'll start to understand much better why people who have things to say to you say the things they do.

Sincere communication has no room for rivalry, dishonesty, or feelings of superiority. And talking down to people is a surefire way of cutting off real communication. The basic core of good relationships is the ability to share. If two people think they have a relationship when, in fact, they can't be honest with each other, they might as well save their breath.

Be Yourself

Jack wants to date Debbie, and when he finally asks her out, all he cares about is that Debbie will like him. As a result, Jack puts on a show. He immediately agrees with everything Debbie mentions, and when she suggests he get involved with the ski club, he agrees.

Months of agony on the slopes may be ahead for Jack; he hates snow and considers his time outside during winter simply as basic survival until spring.

Wanting a relationship is normal. Going against your own feelings and what is important to you, however, only leads to trouble. If Jack could be honest with Debbie and admit he would really like to see her more often, and there must be other things they can share, Debbie might realize she has finally met an honest guy with whom she can also be honest.

If Debbie has the attitude, "Love me, love my skis," then Jack is better off knowing that at the beginning of the relationship. He can decide if Debbie is worth it, and if he really does not care to become a skier, he can begin to look elsewhere for someone else.

Relationships that begin on dishonest terms may seem terrific for a while. If the games never stop, however, only heartache and frustration can result. Save yourself a lot of grief, and be yourself.

Let Your Feelings Flow

Have you ever caught yourself sitting in a parking space, waiting to turn off the car because you want to hear the end of a special song? Join the club. The best songs, the very special ones, create dear memories. Why? Because they say what is deepest and most important to us. They remind us of something special or someone special. These are the songs we have shared with someone we love.

The words make these songs great. Someone, somewhere, feeling the same sensation and daring to risk failure, spent the energy and effort to write these feelings down and try to share them with others.

It is risky to strip away some of your protective shield and actually let others see the "real you." You risk the possibility of rejection and misunderstanding. You risk being hurt. But the only way others can understand what you have to offer is to tell them how you feel. And then the people who reject you, or don't understand you, will walk away. And the ones who are left can become some of your dearest friends.

The only people who are never criticized nor rejected are those who never risk anything. They stay safe and secure behind their walls and seem to be very comfortable. But they will never know the joy of true friendship or the thrill of sharing the beautiful things of life with another person who really understands.

You have the choice—to share your real self with others or to remain isolated. You are the only one who can activate that part of your success. Will you succeed in high school? Yes, if you can break down the barriers you or other people have built and initiate some honest communication.

Rapping It Up

Your life will be as successful as your communication skills allow it to be. In our society, with all its pressures and problems, people need to share some of their feelings with others. Even with chat rooms and E-mail, people are desperately searching for real connections with other people. And the more image and stereotype begin to invade the media, the harder it becomes to be yourself and be honest with others.

With youth on your side, you can begin to turn things around for yourself and the rest of the world. You can start to knock down some of those images and start communicating on a human level.

Start slowly. A smile, a nod, a friendly "hi" will let others know you are not afraid to strike up a casual relationship. Meeting people is half the battle. Once they know you, liking you should be rather easy.

Don't be afraid to talk to adults. They have at most two advantages over you. Some of them may be bigger, and all of them have had more experience. These two things aside, they are simply people trying to live their lives as fully as they can, just as you are. In fact, many adults genuinely fear you, thinking you are smarter or more computer-literate. Some may even fear you will reject them because you may think they are "out of it." By letting them know you are willing to meet them on equal terms and share what you have in common, you can establish the basis of exciting communication, and also become a more mature person.

Grunts and arguments can get some thoughts across. Real words honestly spoken, however, work much better. Try using them!

Points to Ponder

1. How well do your good friends really understand you? Give an example.

_____

_____

2. What do you feel people don't understand about you, and why?

_____

_____

3. How would you rate your ability to participate in a class discussion—and why?

_____

_____

How can it improve?

_____

4. When do you feel the least shy?

_____

Why are you more comfortable in some situations than others?

_____

_____

5. Do you feel you can communicate with adults, and what would make that process easier?

_____

_____

_____

Riding Toward the Future with Your Friends

10

The basketball team has just lost the championship in the last seconds of the game. The cheering section sits, stunned. Parents filter slowly from the stands, trying not to watch the winning team cut down the nets.

In the locker room Mike sits alone. His hair is drenched with perspiration, and his eyes are wet with stinging tears. The agonizing silence seems to keep screaming, "We lost!"

Suddenly a tall shadow falls across the emptiness of that dim locker room. It's Tim, Mike's best friend and teammate, the one who was always there with a joke. Tim reaches out and for a moment touches Mike's shoulders to let Mike know it's okay. This hard time, with two good friends sharing it, is still difficult, but it is also a special time.

Friendship is a very precious thing. Someone once said it is a gift we give ourselves. Your friends are some of the most important people in your life, and if you can enjoy the special things about them, you are fortunate. Friends make life easier, and they are some of your valuable allies as you attempt to make the most of this thing called high school.

Choosing Wisely

"Choose, nothing! I'll take all the friends I can get!" you may say. But do choose wisely. Be aware that when someone becomes your friend, you begin to accept many of that person's likes and dislikes. The attitudes and values of your friends will influence the way you think and evaluate things for many years to come.

Some teens, feeling lonely and left out, make concessions. They are willing to become friends with almost anyone just to make sure they won't be forced to spend night after night at home with their kid brothers and sisters watching reruns.

Others, feeling popularity will make them the envy of classmates, get involved with large groups of people, commonly called cliques. Whatever the reason, many young people, fearing they may miss the best times of their teens, choose friends too lightly. Only later do they have to face some decisions about their choices.

The Circle of Friendship

A common mistake is wanting too many people to be friends with you. Looking at a clique, or even at the varsity football team, you may get the false idea that others have more friends than you. True, these students may have more people who acknowledge them in the halls or cafeteria, but friendship is more than just knowing someone. Having one or two good friends is really worth much more than having a squad of people who simply nod or say hello in the halls.

Our relationships with people happen on many different levels. There are acquaintances who recognize us and sometimes exchange small talk. On another level are casual friends, people with whom we've shared some special moments like involvement in a play or a class. We have certain interests in common with them, like working on the same projects. They may be from our neighborhood, or we may have known them in elementary or middle school. These friends are not, however, those who share the important things.

On the highest level—all by themselves—are those super people, the ones who really know us and still like us. Close friends are always there when we need them. They know what we're trying to say even before we find the words, and they are sincerely honest with us. Those are the best friends at any age. These are the friends who can forget themselves long enough to care about our projects and even our dreams sometimes. They cheer us up when we are down and get honestly excited about our successes. They are selfless enough to care about us almost as much as they care about themselves. One or maybe two good friends are a blessing in anyone's life.

First, Face the Truth

"But I don't need friends," some may say. "I get along by myself. I have friends, sure, but I don't depend on them for anything. I can take care of Number One."

People who talk like this don't have to tell people not to worry about them. No one will! These people don't yet understand that, as the poet John Donne said, "No man is an island." True, people must be able to stand on their own two feet. Because we are social beings, though, we also need each other. You do need people. Believe as strongly as you can that other people need you, too.

If you're feeling that others just don't seem to want your friendship, take a look at yourself. Are you letting people know you respect yourself?

One of the biggest concerns of adults today is the rampant use of drugs by too many of our young people. Do you give in to peer pressure to use alcohol or drugs as a cheap way of winning friends? Or do you rely on alcohol and/or drugs to escape from life's pressures? If you are still caught in the trap of using drugs, take a good look in the mirror. You are worth more than that. Do yourself a favor and start thinking of a better you, and a freer you. Get help from a doctor, a clinic, or a counselor if you need it. If your current friends need drugs to make your friendship work, start looking for real friends who will not be so destructive in your life.

If you are a "poor me" type who sees yourself as nothing but a colossal failure at everything including being a human being, you also communicate that feeling to others. Because no one wants to be around such a negative attitude, people won't want to be around you. We all get into a down mood sometimes, but it may help if you stop and say to yourself, "Wait a minute. Am I this hard on anyone else? Why should I be this hard on me?"

Friendships Grow

To be a good friend, you are expected to be sincere, honest, and generous. You are expected to give up some of your own preferences once in a while.

You cannot hold onto friendship too tightly, and you cannot even define it. Friendships change. Even if someone is a special friend now, don't assume things will remain that way forever. You are changing now, and you will probably change more in the future. As you change, friends may also change. The few good friends who stay with you through the different phases of your life will be most welcome, but don't expect everyone to be part of your life forever.

Friendships grow as people grow, and they change as people change. Good friends who have enough solid understanding between them can grow together. This is the same quality that keeps marriages together. Besides being husband and wife, a man and woman must also be best friends. As their lives change, they must be able to keep up with the changes in themselves and each other. If they cannot, they grow in two different directions, and then trouble sets in.

Be Ready

Sometimes friendships end. Some marriages don't last, either. The reason for this may lie in the fact that two people did not grow together, though at one time they had much in common and could share on different levels. One friend, as his or her own personal life evolves, may develop new interests and new values. The old friendship slowly fades, and things don't seem the same.

If this has not happened to you already, you may just as well brace yourself for the first time it does. Since you and others your age are changing so much, you are bound to develop new interests. And as you mature, some of your values, ideas of entertainment, and attitudes will also change. Your best friend from junior high suddenly may be less friendly, and the two of you may have less to talk about. As a result of these changes, you may drift apart. There will be some pain involved as you go your separate ways. The ending of a friendship is never easy, especially if it was a good friendship. Rather than let the agony of your problem remain and make you uneasy about making other friends, though, just take the good memories of what has been and move on.

Let Your Friend Go Free

There is an old proverb that says, "If you love something, let it go free. If it comes back, it is yours. If not, it never was."

Remember this saying the next time you're tempted to hold too tightly to someone's friendship. You can put your dog on a leash and lock your vehicle in the garage, but your friends must have the freedom to live their own lives. If the two of you can share your experiences and respect each other's individuality, that's great. If not, you may be good acquaintances, but you are not really good friends.

Trying to hold onto a friendship that has already died can only be a cause of heartache. Accept the pain, try to understand why it happened, and move on. There are other people out there, and once they see an opportunity for friendship with you, they'll come in and fill up any emptiness you may feel.

Cliques Are Not the Answer

The clique is that closely knit, super popular, very "in" group. It's the easy way to be sure of steady and good friends. Right?

Wrong.

Cliques have a natural attraction for teens who need a lot of people around them. Belonging to a clique means there will always be someone to call on a rainy Saturday and someone who will eat lunch with you in the cafeteria. Belonging to a clique gives a false feeling of security.

The trouble with cliques is that they keep you from becoming friends with people as individuals. Although they give the illusion that all members know and like each other equally, it is just plain impossible to be best friends with four or five different people! Membership in a clique only tends to stifle each individual's personality and keeps him or her from making deeper friendships that can be more personal and lasting. Adding a new member to a clique is usually impossible, too, because it requires that all members of the group collectively like that person. Almost impossible. And not a good way of ever making new friends, either.

If being popular is that important to you, you may be willing to postpone forming deeper friendships for a time. Sooner or later, however, the need for maturity in your own life will take over. One or two people are bound to strike you as people with whom you could share more. At that point, you will probably either have to give up this possibility or remove yourself from the clique.

Keep the Door Open

High school cliques are nothing more than a carryover from the fifth and sixth grades. That is the stage of child development when it is natural to want to belong to a group. Because children at this age have no developed sense of personal identity, the identity of a group is a good substitute.

As the child moves to adulthood, however, the need for group security should diminish. If it doesn't, you don't really give yourself the chance to learn who you really are as an individual.

There is nothing wrong with having a crowd of friends—your group, your bunch. When your little group starts getting exclusive, though, and you notice others staying away from you because they feel you don't want them around, it's time for a reality check. Is your group being cruel to others? Many teen groups do that. Does your group pick fights with others or spend a great deal of energy putting others down? Then there is something wrong with your group, and staying in it is doing some harmful things to you.

One of the greatest opportunities you have in high school is to meet many different kinds of people. If you lock yourself into a tight group, you deprive yourself of meeting people who may have a lot more in common with you. In fact, they might have become close friends for life, if you had only given them the chance.

Do yourself a favor. Be open to people. Make sure you let others know there is room for them if they want to be your friends.

Most teens have little respect for adults who lock themselves into fixed routines and then stagnate. Don't let the same thing happen to you by closing yourself off from the rest of the world with a selective group of friends.

Can Adults Be Friends?

There's no reason why you can't form friendships with adults. Of course, for safety's sake, these should always be adults you know—not a stranger you meet in a chat room or public place. And if you ever feel an adult is showing too much interest in you, you need to think about where this interest might be leading.

Of course, adults are at different stages of their lives from you, and many of their interests and values differ from yours. But the possibility does remain that a certain teacher, coach, or coworker may strike a responsive chord in you. That can be good. If you can share special problems, or work closely with an adult on a particular project, this may give you an opportunity to get to know him or her in a different way. You may find you can really relate to that person, and you can benefit from knowing him or her.

In the adult world, age has little to do with friendship. By realizing that adults are human too, and that you can share things with them, you can learn early in life that friendship has more to do with what people have in common than with their age or particular roles in life.

Rapping It Up

There are many situations and events that are important in your teen years. People, however, have the greatest power and influence on your life. The people you let into your world, and whom you spend time with, can help make your high school years positive and productive. Real friends can help ease pressure you may feel from home or school.

At the same time, your role as a friend is one of the most important ones you fill. This is as true now as it will be when you are an adult. If you can learn early to be true to yourself and honest with others, you can take a giant step toward a positive and happy life. Cliques can hurt your development as a person; you should choose your friends carefully and individually.

Friends don't exist to continually feed your ego or back up your every decision, right or wrong. There are always difficult times when two personalities conflict, and you may sometimes feel your friends ask too much of you.

Someone wrote once that friendship is a sacrament that should be taken on one's knees. This was a symbolic way of saying that friendship is almost blessed, and it should be very precious and dear in our lives. Friendships are not prizes we win. They are gifts that should be appreciated and nurtured.

Caring and loving is the name of the game. If you can forget your own needs once in a while, and really give part of yourself to another person in honest friendship, you will be able to live up to the standards of true, good relationships. You will also learn how terrific it is to give as well as to take.

Sometime up ahead in your life, you may come to love one person in a special way. The quality of that love you finally are capable of giving in marriage will come partly from the quality of love you learn to give in friendship.

If you don't learn anything else in high school, learn how to be a true friend. You need friendship and so do the people who will be sharing the best and worst times of your life. You are unique and special. Being a good friend to others can make you even more special!

Points to Ponder

1. What qualities about you make you a good friend?

_____

_____

2. How much will you go along with others just to keep their friendship? Be specific.

_____

_____

3. What qualities do you look for in a friend?

_____

_____

4. What do you think holds a real friendship together?

_____

_____

5. Explain your own opinion of cliques and why they exist.

_____

_____

_____

The Home Front

There's that voice, that very familiar voice, bellowing from the vague direction of the kitchen. "If you don't get out of bed this minute, you'll be late."

Here you go. Another day. Another run-through of all your classes and another chance to face all the pressures that rear their ugly heads. And where does it all begin? At home.

Surviving what happens at school, to no one's surprise, can be made easier or more difficult by the help, or lack of it, that comes from home. Problems at home can affect your whole life. Your success and happiness at home can mean the difference between life being a first-class pain or something that is really enjoyable.

Understanding the Folks

Your parents never had a class in high school called Parenting 101. And there is no set of standards for achieving super parenthood. Most couples resign themselves to learning how to be good parents on the job, by trial and error.

Before you say that your folks must be setting the all-time record for errors, try to understand their situation. We have already said that it is hard for your folks to keep up with the changes in your life—as well as the changes in the world since they were your age. Rapid technological advances in the new century are something they never had to contend with. They grew up in a simpler time. While you are at home on the Internet and bouncing around chat rooms and E-mail, this is all new to your parents, who managed to develop relationships and communication without the Web.

Even if you are not the first-born child, you are not a carbon copy of your older brothers and sisters. Because of this, you present a whole new set of problems for Mom and Dad. They never really know what to expect from you. Once they think they do, you pull an about-face and zap them with a whole new way of acting!

If you can understand this, you may be able to understand your parents' reactions a bit better. They need help to understand you, and this is where you can make yourself part of the solution instead of part of the problem. You can give them that help.

Parents Aren't Perfect

The biggest problem you face with your parents is that they're adults. They are the ultimate authority figures in your life, and have power over you. The state and legal authorities think you are not mature yet. They may be wrong, but they feel you are not responsible for all your actions. So they give your folks a lot of rights and responsibilities over your life.

This position gives some teens a bitter opinion of their parents, whom they view as enemies standing in the way of freedom and independence. When these teens feel their freedom is threatened or held back, they get resentful, and resent the people who make it happen. But this doesn't have to be so.

You and your parents can grow to understand each other better. They should realize that you are a person on the move, a person who is maturing in many different ways—from your body to your values and abilities. Your parents should also realize this is their time to begin letting you go. They have to let you test your wings, fall on your face a few times, and finally learn to soar off on an independent and productive life of your own.

You, on the other hand, have to accept the fact that your parents have been your mainstay all these years. Letting go is a painful process. Your folks have really enjoyed watching you grow, despite any growing pains your family has experienced. You are a part of your parents, and while they may not be thrilled about all the bills your presence has added to the family, they have enjoyed your uniqueness and the special times your presence in the family has meant. Now that they see many of these things coming to an end as you embark on a new phase of your life after high school, they may have some very mixed emotions.

Parents want the best for their children. They want you to be successful and happy. Because of this, your folks are cautious of situations that may be harmful to you. Fearing you might make some gigantic mistakes and wrong decisions, they set rules, guidelines, and yes, even punishments. Your parents may not be happy about grounding you or depriving you of things, but they are acting from the obligation to do what is best for you, which includes impressing upon you right and wrong ways of acting. If you can understand and begin to respond to your folks in a positive way, chances are they will grant you more freedom and respect in return.

Freedom Means No Sides

At this point you my be wondering, "Whose side on you on, anyway?"

The truth is, there should be no sides.

The family has always been spoken of as a circle. As in a circle, there are no sides in a family. There are only people—and all of them are on the inside.

The adversarial relationship that creeps into too many families comes when any or all of the family members fail to work together. Selfishness may make you aware of only your side of any problem, and your parents may be equally entrenched in their own views. When individuals fail to sit down and honestly appreciate all aspects of a problem, they begin to argue and make demands, turning a home into a battleground.

How can you avoid confrontation in your home? You can't. How you attempt to handle that confrontation, however, marks how far you have come along the road to maturity.

Communication Is the Key

There's that word again—communication! You may think it's impossible to communicate with your parents. You may feel your folks are not interested in your life. They may be up to their ears in their own problems and worries, and because of the time pressures they feel, they may have little opportunity to sit down and talk. Your parents may also be aware of your growing independence, and they may be trying to give you a little room to test your wings. They may not want to appear snoopy, so they may be waiting for you to be the first to talk about certain friends or situations.

Whatever the reasons for the lack of communication, the time to start talking to your parents is now! If you think your parents are uninterested in you, make them interested. Tell them what is important to you, what has you upset, and what worries you. Don't be afraid to make everyone at home aware of what's going on in your life. Tell them about your classes, about that English teacher who upsets you, about the discussion you had during lunch. Tell them why you like your particular kind of music, and about your favorite websites. Tell them why you wouldn't be caught dead wearing the outfit your aunt gave you for Christmas. Running the risk of boring your family is much better than running the risk of losing them due to a lack of communication.

You don't need to sit in your room all evening. There is something happening around the house—make yourself part of it. If you are not afraid to share with family members, your parents may soon begin sharing their problems and lives with you.

If you think your parents don't care, make them care. They may have reached the point where they are afraid to show some honest affection, or they may be taking you for granted. They may also be fighting their own fights with depression, alcohol or drug abuse, or unhappiness in their jobs.

Love your parents. Don't be afraid to let them know they have a special place in your heart, and let them know you are aware of problems they may be having. Don't be afraid to give a little hug once in a while. When you were a child, you expected the world to come to you with love and interest. If you really are on your way to adulthood, act like a person who is becoming an adult. Take the initiative. Make the first move.

Some people feel awkward about touching and showing affection. But if you cannot show affection in your own way to your family, you're not living your life to the fullest!

Split-Level Love

There may be problems at home. Your parents may have marital problems, and you may be suffering, too. You may be living with only one of your parents because divorce has split your original family apart. Your family may include stepparents, stepbrothers, and stepsisters. A member of your family may have died, or you may have a grandparent living with you. There are a variety of situations that may have touched your family, as they are touching millions of others.

You are not alone. Teens today are dealing more often with divorce and remarriage. It helps to remember that people for generations have dealt with these situations, and they have managed to survive and have productive, happy lives.

You first need to understand that any breakups in your family are not your fault. Differences between your mother and father are *theirs*. By trying to understand these differences, you can help each of them move on and make the most of their lives. But in no way should you let the failure of their marriage be a failure for you. It is, in fact, an opportunity for you to show your growing maturity by trying to understand.

If you are now living in a family restructured by remarriage, realize this present group is also your family in every sense of the word. Your stepparent needs your efforts at acceptance. Your stepbrothers and stepsisters also deserve to be part of your life. Be big enough to accept them under the roof and into your heart. They, too, are going through a difficult adjustment, and they need to know that everyone is making an effort toward becoming a new and caring family.

You should also try to get over being angry with your parents, if they are divorced or if you have any other "baggage" with them. If your parents have hurt you, be strong enough to forgive them. No one ever expected them to be perfect when they started out, just as no one is expecting perfection from you.

One of the most difficult things to realize at this young time of your life is that your parents are human. Because of their own growth and change as individuals, they may no longer be able to share their lives with each other. This is extremely hard to accept, and it is a lot to ask of you. It may, however, be asked of you. Now it is your turn to respond to the situation by showing as much strength and caring as you can.

Once you recognize your parents as human beings and face the reality of their individuality, you can still love them. You may even be living apart from one or both of them. But they are still family, and they always will be. If you can enjoy your good memories and think of your parents in a positive way all through your life, you will have a richness no one can ever destroy.

Families are for sharing. If you are going to share the good, you are also expected to share the bad. It is never easy, but sad times are part of every individual's growth as a person. If you do your best to work through them, you will develop a sense of strength and accomplishment you can carry with you into your adult life.

Brothers and Sisters

Your brothers and sisters can present a real problem for you, or they can be a real joy. Sure, you may resent your older brother because he seems to have had it so much easier than you. You may even resent the way your little stepsister keeps interrupting you when your friends are over or when you're trying to work or listen to music.

Living with someone isn't the easiest thing in the world. In the case of brothers and sisters, there is always the temptation to compare how they are treated with how you think you are making out. You may think they get their way more than you do. Yet passing up the chance to develop a good relationship with brothers and sisters may be one of the biggest mistakes you can make. If you can keep yourself on good terms with your brothers and sisters now, you may find they can become unique friends when you are all adults. Your older brother may be a good friend and ally in years to come. Your little stepsister, once she is a woman, may be a source of pride and sincere joy for you.

By sharing your own successes and interests in school, you can help your younger brothers and sisters have a better attitude toward education. Also, by confiding in your older brothers and sisters, you can learn a lot and make them feel useful.

Rapping It Up

The school has an open house, and only a handful of parents appear. Why? There may be many answers. Mom and Dad are too busy. Or they may not care. Or they would have come, but you never told them about it.

Your home life and your school life are wound up in an interesting and complicated maze. You can try to keep the two parts of your life separate and never share a word about one with the other. But it can be useful to help your teachers understand you better by letting them in on some of the aspects of your home life. You can also make home an easier place to come back to by not keeping what happens in school a military secret.

Your parents are human. They have their own lives, and they are unique individuals. They are also the people who have the greatest possibility of influencing your life. If you let them, their influence can be substantial.

Do you realize that your ties to home can be your biggest asset during high school? Honest communication with your folks can give your home life a whole new dimension. It can also give you some valuable help with your problems.

If there are walls between you and your parents, or between you and your brothers and sisters, tear them down. You may actually be the one who will turn things around at home and make everyone else more open and caring as well as more interested in each other.

You are not a kid anymore. Begin to assume a bit more responsibility on the home front by taking the initiative when things need to get done and by accepting responsibility for some of the family's concerns. These actions will go a long way toward proving to your parents that you are becoming a mature adult.

Your folks are watching you and waiting. Every hint that you are turning into a more open and dependable individual is a joy to them. By sharing with them, you can help them understand how you're doing and give them some clues to help you become a better person.

Home is where the heart is. You will love many other people and things in your life, but you should always leave room for your family. Building good relationships with your family will help you have better relations with others as you enter the adult world on your own.

Points to Ponder

1. How much emotional support do you get from your family? Explain.

_____

_____

_____

2. What are your parents' biggest concerns right now?

_____

_____

_____

3. How open are you with your parents? How much do you share with them?

_____

_____

Give an example of something you are honest with them about or something you are not honest about.

_____

_____

_____

4. How important is home to you?

_____

5. How different will your own home be when you have a family? Be specific.

_____

_____

_____

_____

_____

The Free Spirit in Free Time

"Don't bother opening up the curtain for my social scene," you might say. "There's no one on the stage!"

What most people would call your social life, and what you might sometimes feel like calling a disaster, includes all that time when you're pretty much your own boss. True, you have homework, family responsibilities, and curfews, but how you fill up free hours is becoming more and more your own decision.

There does come a joyous time when the last class is over, and you can head into the rest of your life. You are free at last. You are on your own, and you finally have a chance to do what you want!

Hard as a Rock Concert

What you choose for entertainment says much about you. The people you spend time with also have an effect on you.

Entertainment means more to you than it does to many adults. They have more things to fill up their lives, and their free time is limited. Most adults face responsibilities, pressures, and concerns from which you are still relatively free. Entertainment for adults is really a time to escape from their problems and relax.

Teens, however, because they are so involved with peer pressure and because they cannot escape the fact that their lives are changing, tend to think of their social lives as something to enjoy, but also something to work on. Don't fall into the trap of forcing yourself to have fun or be happy. Relaxing is the first key to really enjoying your free time.

For you, being where the action is means being active. For example, most adults would not choose a rock concert for entertainment. But look at yourself at that concert! What a sight! Are you going to sit back and just let all that good music go to waste? Absolutely not! There you are—dancing, clapping, singing, and getting so involved with it all that no one can tell where the music stops and you start. You love really getting into it, and you love every minute!

It's great that you can enjoy that special spark inside you that makes you act this way. Just don't *make* yourself do it. The first answer to entertainment is being yourself.

Hanging Out or Hanging In

Of course, not all your time is going to be spent at organized entertainment functions such as dances, movies, and concerts. You probably can't afford it, and besides, there is a lot to be said for just hanging out with your friends.

Don't be afraid to just spend time with your friends. You need these free times, when you are not facing any pressures of role or image. You probably know some adults who are so caught up in their roles that they can't be themselves. If they could just sit back, as you should, and let their friends accept them for what they are, they might be better off.

Be careful not to fall into the trap of image, even in your free time. If you feel you have to be seen in the right places with the right people, doing the right things, you may be winning points in the popularity poll, but you may not be true to yourself. You may not be truly happy, either. Your free-time activities show you very clearly as you really are. Let them be natural and unpressured.

Surfing the Web

With computers now a fixture in so many American homes, teens often use much of their free time exploring the vast expanse of the Internet. While homework assignments and other demands drive you to the Web, the Internet has also become a large part of many teens' free time.

There are many things to consider before you use the Internet, however. Chat rooms can be fun, but they can also be dangerous. Their anonymity gives access to anyone who wants to tap into your life—but only if you let them. The word here is caution. Go ahead and use chat rooms, but keep in mind these are people you really don't know. Looking someone in the eyes is one feature the Internet can't give you. Be careful when you surf!

E-mail also takes up a lot of teens' time. It offers a great opportunity to keep in contact with friends who have moved away, people you've met at conferences or over the summer, and even friends across town. Again, the word is caution.

These days there are websites for everything, and as a teen you have access to them all. Using the Internet is one chance for you to prove your maturity and your own sense of growing responsibility. Use the Web well and you can learn and grow a lot. Use the dregs of the Web, and that's exactly where you end up, in the dregs.

You grew up with computer games, and they're getting better all the time. But remember that games are a form of entertainment and that the time and emphasis you give them should be in balance with the other aspects of your life. All time spent at the computer should be a help to you, so keep your various activities on it in perspective.

The Internet is a tool, and while it can offer you entertainment as well as information, it can also become an obsession. It shouldn't take away the time you spend with friends. People need human contact, and you can't replace your friends with hours alone in front of a computer. In this new century, with advances appearing all the time, it will be your own sense of maturity and responsibility that determines how the Web will affect not only you, but many members of your generation. You are in the computer generation. Make that a positive statement.

The School Connection

Some teens feel they are living on an island, with nothing to do and no one to share their time. If you feel this way, look back to the discussion in Chapter 8 on extracurricular involvement.

Part of your education can be found in books, but a big part is in the things you do outside the classroom. This includes the many activities sponsored by the school that are either free or very economical. If you feel there is nothing to do in the evenings, get involved in a play, a club, or a special school activity. It could also put you in contact with some interesting and stimulating people.

Your social life can get its biggest push from your connection with school and the people you meet there. Don't be afraid to give it a try.

Dating or Waiting?

"When should I start dating? What's the right age? How do I know when I'm ready?"

No one can answer those questions for you. There are, of course, many people who will try. Your folks may have some very definite ideas about it. Your teachers may offer advice, and certainly your friends will put the pressure on you to move ahead into this possibly exciting time of your life. But when is the right time for you? Only you know for sure.

Some parents, wanting success for their children in all areas of their lives, will push sons and daughters to date very early. They may feel they missed out on the action when they were young and want their children to have the fun and popularity they missed. Other parents fear the worst and want to keep their children on the shelf until they reach twenty!

Some good, honest discussion with your folks may help get these issues settled. Whatever you do, don't let yourself be pushed into doing anything until you feel it is right for you. Your parents will get over the fact that right now you may be more interested in other things, or in dealing with members of the opposite sex in a group or more casual way. They will also still survive that fateful night when you do walk out the front door on your first date. There will probably have to be some compromises on both sides, but your dating life should grow directly out of your readiness for it and your honest desire to begin dating.

Your peers, the crowd at school, may also try to force their own ideas on you. If they think you should be dating, but you just don't feel like it, let them know in an independent but kind way that you are still thinking about it. If they are your real friends, they will back off and leave you alone on that subject for a while.

Inventory

Choose the answers that best describe you.

_____ I need someone to be there just for me.

_____ My parents don't understand what I need.

_____ Dating is my right whenever I choose.

_____ I've got to get out of the house, and this is my answer.

_____ It's time I got sexually active, so why not?

_____ My friends date, so I might as well, too.

Dancing Queen—or Turning Green?

Ah, that first date!

Dan is there, spiffed up until his hair squeaks. Debbie comes down the stairs, her eyes full of expectation. And they are off for the evening.

Mom and Dad watch them drive away, thinking back to their own teen years. Dad immediately buries his head in the paper. He's not reading it; he's trying to cope with the fact his little girl has just walked out the door.

At the restaurant Dan is the epitome of politeness, and Debbie, after ordering, sits anxiously back and looks at him.

Silence. Very horrible, awkward silence! Now what? Panic time! What to say???

Cheer up. Your first date, or your first meeting with anyone who has the potential of becoming special to you, will have its awkward moments. The possibilities are so great, and the situation so new, that it will always take a little time to adjust. But that old standby, communication, will come to your aid again. Sure, you may have to ask some foolish, seemingly superficial questions. You may even end up giving a dissertation on a class at school. Eventually, however, you will loosen up if you are both talking.

Silence is a beautiful thing when it happens between two people who know each other so well they can be comfortable with it. Until that happens, words are going to be your best bet. Disc jockeys fight to avoid the number-one disaster in radio—dead air. Nothing is being said or sung. It is considered a failure for them.

A handy trick for avoiding dead air yourself until you can learn to share meaningful silence with someone you know is to try learning about the other person's interests. Ask *why* and *how* questions that will require more than a yes or no answer. Sooner or later the ice will break. If the communication is open and honest, you both should begin to have a good time.

Dating Can Ruin Your Social Life

How can this be?

Take a moment to think about your total social life, which includes all those faithful friends who were the mainstay of your free time before Mr. or Miss Wonderful came along. Some teens, once they start dating, quickly forget their old friends and neglect them. This, of course, is one of the surest ways of missing out on a lot of fun. It also marks you as a friend who will be around only until something better comes along.

It is possible to date and still maintain a schedule for doing things with your other friends from time to time. The more you become involved with one person, the more difficult it will be to maintain this balance. However, it's important to try. You owe it to yourself, and you owe it to the friends who have stood by you when things weren't as rosy as they may be now.

Exclusive Property?

Many teens today feel that once they begin dating, they cannot, or must not, even look at another member of the opposite sex. But going out with a person a few times does not mean he or she owns you.

Possessiveness is just a way of keeping a kind of social security. In most cases, teens in exclusive relationships are not really preparing for marriage. Some are simply making sure that they have a date for the big dance or that Saturday night will not be a popcorn fest with a little brother.

Some more mature couples realize this and loosen up in their relationships and agree to date other people. If you can handle this, do it. The teen years are a time for finding out what life has to offer. It usually is not wise to plan your future around the first person you date. Perhaps some marriages fail because the partners did not date enough in their teens. They got so involved with each other so early that they never really learned of others who could also have been good life partners. You may even ask that question of your own parents if they have divorced.

Group dating, an arrangement that was common several decades ago, has also found a way back into popularity. It involves a group of boys and girls meeting at one place and having a good time together. There is no great emphasis on pairing off. It is just an open evening of fun. Eventually, of course, couples may begin to form, and people may drift in and out of the group. However, for a while, this arrangement gives everyone a chance to get to know many different kinds of people. It also helps you make some decisions about one-to-one dating with a little more intelligence and understanding. Try it. You might like it.

Is Sex Part of Dating?

That's a question you must answer for yourself. Popular music and films, as well as locker room discussions, all tell you sex is usually a part of dating. But truly honest people will tell you it isn't.

While we'll talk about sexual involvement in a later chapter, let's say this much right now. Society seems to say that sex is all right for anyone, anytime. In too many high schools and colleges, young people give the impression that it is as common an occurrence as going to a restaurant. They may tell you sex is the natural ending to any night of socializing.

They are wrong. And they are wrong not just because AIDS is a real concern. As the new century begins, there has been a sober acknowledgment of the risks involved with AIDS and other sexually transmitted diseases. This has led to a real rethinking about sexual involvement for many people of all ages. Sexual involvement before marriage still violates many people's religious beliefs. For all, the *assumption* of sex is wrong, simply because no one can tell a healthy, independent person what he or she should do. This is a personal decision—don't let your peers make it for you.

Many young people even stop dating because they don't want to constantly fight off the pressure for sex. When you do start dating, show your maturity and growth of independence by your actions. Dating does not mean going to bed with anyone who has given you a meal, smiled at you nicely, or told you you're special.

Be really special. Be your own person, and make your own decisions.

Rapping It Up

Your friends can be the source of much fun and real enjoyment. You can even learn to have some good times with your family if you are open and communicative at home. And your school is set up to provide many activities you can enjoy after regular class hours.

In fact, your whole life can become a source of real pleasure and fulfillment—if you let it. Being open with others and honest with yourself is the key.

Dating can give you valuable experience in learning how to handle personal relationships. It can open your eyes to the wonderful world of caring in a special way, and it can make you more aware of yourself as a worthwhile individual.

Take advantage of your youth, however, and before you decide to date only one person, consider the fact that dating in high school is an excellent opportunity to find out what—and who—is out there. Part of the reason for dating is to open yourself up to the possibilities of really understanding the opposite sex and finding what different individuals have to offer.

Just remember to let dating, and your social life in general, come easily and comfortably for you. Don't let anyone pressure you into doing things that make you feel uncomfortable.

If you can learn to smile at life, you may soon find it smiling back at you. Enjoy!

Points to Ponder

1. How much does the entertainment you choose reflect the real you?

_____

_____

2. Are you able to forget your image and really be yourself when you are out for the evening?

_____

Why or why not?

_____

_____

3. How can you keep your old friends once you start dating on a fairly regular basis?

_____

_____

_____

4. Can you be yourself on a date, or do you feel you must always please the other person? Explain.

_____

_____

_____

5. What are your own attitudes toward sexual involvement?

_____

_____

_____

_____

A Sporting Chance

13

Five seconds left on the clock. The score is tied! Wait, there goes the quarterback! He's going to pass! It's long, long. Murphy is there. He's reaching. Yes! Touchdown! The crowd goes wild!

Sports can be like that, especially if you're Murphy, but sports can be very different, too. There is a lot of glory on a playing field, a basketball court, or track. Some teens, thinking they can get a piece of it, sign up for a team. Participating in any sport, however, also involves a lot of behind-the-scenes work and hours of lonely, hard training. The few minutes of individual glory that may follow are never a sure thing. Often the person who goes out for a team just to win the praise of others does not last too long.

Is It Worth It?

That is a question only you can answer. Participating in your high school sports program offers many opportunities for growth, if you are willing to pay the price. Working at sports—and it certainly is work and not play—can tone up your body while also toning up your mind. The training and sense of dedication that will be demanded of you will teach you how to give yourself to a worthy goal. By competing, you can learn the valuable lesson that *trying* is often more rewarding than any victory that may come.

No athlete who is worthy of continued support looks at glory as the goal. To excel in sports, a person must really enjoy putting out the best effort at all times. He or she knows the personal satisfaction that can come from reaching individual goals. Even though an athlete works hard to win, the most important winning goes on inside the person. It is the personal best, not the all-time best, that really counts.

Whether or not you decide to participate in high school sports will depend heavily on your own evaluation of what is important. You have only so much time. If sports is that important to you, then make the commitment to do it well.

The Pressure to Win

Ron is out for football. He enjoys it. His dad, his number-one fan, is behind him 100 percent. Dad tries to make as many practice sessions as he can. And when a game is coming up, he helps Ron review the patterns and plays, as well as the scouting reports.

Sounds great, right? Yet when Ron fumbles the football during the big game, and the home team goes on to lose by a touchdown, it is not Ron, but Dad, who goes to pieces. "How could he do that? My son? How could he do that to me?" Ron, like many other teens, is getting too much pressure from the home front.

Many students, both boys and girls, choose not to go out for sports in high school because they feel they can't take the pressure, either from their own parents or from other sources.

Teens realize it is only a game, but in some areas of the country and in some school districts, there is much pressure to be the best. Rather than get involved with that kind of pressure, some teens stay away from competitive sports.

In some school systems where athletics are overly stressed, pride in the team is seen as a way for parents and taxpayers to view something tangible about the high school. Some school officials feel that if the rugged football team is not winning, the high school as a whole is not winning, no matter what test scores and college entrance ratios say.

When parents of school athletes or school personnel make winning conference titles and championships the most important thing, trophy fever is quickly transmitted to the coaches and players. Tension builds. Look at the frequency with which coaches at some schools change jobs. If they last only a few years, you can be sure there is pressure from somewhere to win, and win big.

The secret of participating in varsity sports, where this pressure will always be present to some degree, is to let it remain in the background as an incentive to do better. It should never overshadow the real purpose of the sporting program. If some adults in the community get upset about losing once in a while, that is their problem. Don't let it become yours.

The importance of sports is always a good question for debate. Some teens feel it is treated like the only thing going on in the school. Others feel it is not given enough support. The way you feel about this issue may change during your high school career, but traveling the middle road will always give you the best perspective. No one thing is all important in high school. The whole concept of secondary education lies in providing as many experiences as possible for as many people as possible. If sports is your interest, then go for it, and give it the best you can.

If you choose not to participate on the varsity level, there are always less-pressured sports that compete for more enjoyment and do not carry the reputation of the school athletic program on their backs.

Team Player?

If you decide to become involved in sports, you will have to decide on the type of competition you desire. The sports that usually capture much of the glory, and much of the fans' money, are the team efforts. Basketball and football remain the two favorites in most high schools, with swimming, hockey, and soccer gaining support in different parts of the country.

Team sports involve a particular kind of pressure. Each individual has his or her own assignment and becomes a specialist. An athlete plays one position or participates in only one or two events. He or she then must concentrate on a very narrow aspect of the total game. A player tries to be outstanding in his or her unique job.

The greatest satisfaction for you as a team player, if you decide to become involved, will be to learn to work with others for a common goal—victory. Team efforts will continue on many different levels throughout your life, such as in your job and in your family. If you can learn to sacrifice yourself once in a while for the greater good of the group, you will have learned a lot!

It's All on Me

"I'd rather be in a sport where I can control everything. In each event, I am the only one I have to worry about. I know that if I can do everything as well as I can, I have a good chance of winning. Each time I compete against my own performance at the last meet. This way I know if I'm getting any better."

A state champion in gymnastics said that, and her feelings are echoed by successful men and women who participate in singles tennis, weightlifting, wrestling, golf, and other individual sports. These sports demand another kind of training. In these games you will be expected to learn all the aspects of the sport and become a total player. When the competition begins, it is you who will succeed or fail. Some teens find the pressure of these sports a bit much to handle. If something goes wrong, there is no one else to blame.

This kind of pressure requires individuals who are confident enough to go out and attempt their best. Very few teens who participate in individual sports are shy or have personality problems. They have to be in control of their emotions as well as their bodies. These athletes must really have their act together, both mentally and physically.

If you choose to try out for a sport that will put you all alone against the rest of the world, you know something about yourself. You are not afraid of failure. You are a

confident and psychologically strong individual, or you
soon will be!

Consider the Alternatives

While many teens choose not to get involved with varsity
sports, they still take advantage of sports as a hobby or
just a fun activity. From tennis lessons to intramural
games, sports still have much to offer. Consider joining a
bowling league in your neighborhood, or studying gymnastics or modern dance at a local studio. Jogging, power
walking, and roller blading are popular sports that you can
take into your adult life. In northern areas, cross-country
skiing or other winter sports provide hours of fun with
people who share your interests. There are many teens
who get into the habit of working out, either in a weight or
an aerobics program at a local fitness center. An interest
in exercise is not only good now. It will give you a healthy
attitude toward your body that can continue into your
adult life.

Just remember that you don't have to be part of the
varsity program at school to enjoy sports. Find what's good
for you, and enjoy it!

Warning

From professional sports programs through the college and
high school level, there exists a feeling among some star
athletes that they have certain privileges others don't
have. Some of these presumed privileges include taking
liberty with the opposite sex, demanding special attention
on personal matters, or changing grades to make passing a
class possible.

Sports stars enjoy the adulation and support of fans.
But the athlete must learn to handle success *gracefully*.
Those who star in high school must also learn to keep the
adulation and attention in perspective, because once high
school is over, stardom may not continue. Perhaps those
people simply experience their own fifteen minutes of fame
very early in their lives. The rest of life is what matters.
And it all has to be lived in perspective.

Rapping It Up

There are many levels of sporting competition available in high school. Even in gym class, you will have a chance to learn aspects of different sports. You may develop an interest in some sports that will last for years to come.

Sandlot games and intramural competition are a lot of fun. Individual sports such as bowling, tennis, and running offer healthy and enjoyable recreation. They can give you a good workout without the pressure that comes with highly visible varsity teams.

High school is your big job right now. It is there for developing the total you. Whether you are fond of it or not, your body will be with you all your life. If you don't give it a chance to develop through healthy exercise during your teens, you may find it wearing out on you much sooner than you had expected.

Participation in sports can also help you learn to use your leadership abilities well. Many high schools look to athletes for initiative and leadership, because they know these people know how to face challenges.

If you choose to become involved in high school sports programs, give them your best. Also, remember the pressure is only a tool that can help you give even more than you thought possible.

If, on the other hand, you decide sports are not for you, don't judge those who participate. Athletes are proving to themselves and the rest of the world that they can be a success. They are asserting their individuality by putting their effort on the line and striving for victory. If some of your friends elect to dedicate themselves to the discipline of sports, respect the courage and stamina they show, and give them your support.

You can, of course, expect the same kind of respect from your sports-minded friends when you get involved in drama, band, journalism, or debate. High school is really one big team, and if you can learn to pull together with everyone—respecting them for their individuality and asserting yourself at the same time—you can work through any prejudices or pressures that may come along. All it takes is remembering to be a good sport!

Points to Ponder

1. Do you feel capable of the real dedication it takes to participate in sports? Why?

_____

_____

2. Explain why you do or don't like sports.

_____

_____

3. How do you handle defeat—in sports or other events? Explain.

_____

_____

4. It takes a lot of faith in one's ability to enter competition. How much faith in yourself do you have?

_____

_____

5. If you do not participate in sports, are you open-minded toward the people who do? If you do participate, are you supportive of those in other extracurricular activities? Explain.

_____

_____

_____

The Battle for the Buck

14

Bill has a few minutes alone in the locker room before the rest of the class comes in. Suddenly he realizes that a lot of money-filled wallets are lying around, unprotected and very vulnerable.

The opportunity is there. Chances are Bill may not be caught, and there is that CD he was looking at in the store just last weekend. Tempting. Very tempting. What will our man Bill do? What would you do?

No one will deny having money is important. Having it—or not having it—may determine what others think of us. The need for money may add to the tension at home. And it may force us to pass up participation in after-school activities in order to work at a part-time job.

Money! Money! Money!

Everyone needs money. How do you get it, and what is enough for you?

Teens who are too young to be hired in the business world are often frustrated. Baby-sitting can be one alternative for teens with empty pockets. Other enter-prising teens investigate the opportunities for offering lawn care and housecleaning services in their area.

Unfortunately, some people consider stealing another possibility. No high school administrator can say his or her school is free from theft. In fact, stealing is the number-one crime committed by teens. In older buildings, it is easy to break into lockers. Many students are careless with purses and wallets. As a result, the temptation to steal is almost unbearable for some students.

If you ever face such a temptation—you need money and you see an easy way to get it—let your conscience be the final judge. Your own values will make the right answer clear.

How you act depends solely on you. No one can make a rule you will obey or set a guideline you will follow if you first cannot set your own values right. Religion, strict parents, or watchful teachers can't control you. You can, and do, make all your own decisions. You also live with them.

One of the most essential things to develop during high school is a realistic and honest attitude toward money. Money is a tool, and that's all. True, it is a handy tool to have around, but if it becomes more than that in your mind, you may end up being a very frustrated and miserable human being.

"Just in Case"

As a high school student, do you need money in your pockets? Of course you do. If you or your friends have parents who don't believe it, be sure you let them know what real life is all about. As you mature, you need to feel you are developing your own independence. Having money can help that feeling of being able to handle your own life.

You should be able to feel the security of knowing that you will not be embarrassed by being unable to meet the little needs that can appear. There may be a new paper-back you need for English class, or your friends may decide to stop for a snack after school. It doesn't have to be much money, but you should feel the confidence of knowing you can handle most normal money demands.

The *amount* of money you carry, of course, is another story. If you feel you need fifty dollars in your pocket "just in case," you may be spending too much money. Several dollars will usually do the trick. Watching those dollars disappear will make you think twice before you decide you really need something. It may also teach you to look for bargains.

How Much Is Enough?

You may be very aware of a member of your crowd who always has a lot of money. This person is willing to pay for that after-school burger, and whenever he or she opens up that wallet, it makes you feel like a pauper.

Some teens whose parents are well off carry large amounts of cash. They may use money as an image builder, and they may derive some of their confidence in social situations from their ability to pay. However, most teens don't have the opportunity to build their images in this manner. Actually, they're better off. Relying on money for friendship or prestige is a trap in which many adults are caught, too. If you can avoid this trap while you are young, so much the better.

There is no set amount of allowance that is right for everyone. Some areas of the country are more expensive than others. Also, some teens face more financial pressures than others. Your biggest consideration should be what your family can afford and what they think is appropriate. As a small child, you may have had an unrealistic idea of how much money the family had. You usually got what you wanted, and there always seemed to be a few extra dollars in your mother's purse. Part of growing up, however, is coming to terms with your family's financial situation.

If you want to get a more realistic idea of what kind of allowance you can expect, or if your family needs all its income for basic expenses, try having a good, honest talk with your parents about finances. Your parents may be having a hard time paying the rent or mortgage each month. In addition, prices keep rising. They may be saving for your college years, which involves enormous expenses. Understanding some of your parents' expenses will give you a better appreciation of what they are facing.

Your folks may already be cutting back on their own expenses. This may prompt you to rethink your lifestyle. If this is the case, you should try to understand and imitate their example since you are now a more mature, responsible member of the family. It may also lead you to consider college or trade school as a necessity after high school, because statistics show that higher education almost guarantees higher earning power as an adult. Think about that.

What About a Job?

Are part-time jobs good for teens? That's a good question with a complicated answer.

Some parents don't want their sons or daughters to work while they are in high school. They feel their schoolwork might suffer. Others, facing the straining family budget, honestly tell their children a little extra added income would help. These parents encourage their teens to find jobs to help defray their own expenses.

Teens' needs tend to get more expensive, too. Buying a small toy for Heather when she was a child was a piece of cake. Now that Heather wants new sound equipment and some updates on the family computer, or a computer of her own, things get more complicated.

Part-time jobs do have benefits. Some teens feel they learn a lot by working. Book knowledge gives a basis for thinking about future career possibilities. But the experience gained from slinging hamburgers gives more confidence to handle real-life situations. Jobs also give young people a chance to work with others of different ages and backgrounds. They also offer the opportunity to become involved in the work world, with all its challenges, frustrations, and rewards.

One danger of working is the possibility that your study time will be reduced. Work may also cut into your valuable free time. If your job makes your life so hectic that you are running home from school, giving your homework a lick and a promise, and then rushing off to a job, you are missing a very important time in your life. You need time to hang loose—to relax. If you don't get relaxation time, you may join the thousands of teens who are trying to get rid of ulcers. If your job creates that kind of pressure, it's not worth it.

Teachers complain that too many teens who work long hours come to school with little sleep, and then fall asleep in class. What suffers is the most important job of their lives—their schoolwork.

You Owe Yourself

Teens usually work very hard and get paid minimum wage or even less. They are often the last to be hired and the first to be fired. They are at rock bottom on the pay scale. If you can face this and still work for the extra money you may feel will make your life more comfortable, go to it. Just don't let a job get in the way of what is important in your life. Your education and your growth as a person should always come first.

The dazzle of a fairly large paycheck has driven many teens out of school before graduation. Most soon found out, though, that they were making money but were stuck in jobs with little opportunity for advancement. Without a high school diploma, they faced a lifetime of really hard work.

Stay in school. Work if you must, but keep your priorities straight. You owe yourself the chance to make the most of your potential. Your education is your big job right now. Believe in the payoff it will bring.

Rapping It Up

There are a lot of well-dressed adults who may make you green with envy because they drive expensive cars and project a successful image. Although they may be pleased with themselves and their possessions, some of these people have little else of real satisfaction in their lives. They may be hung up on material things, on possessing things, on working hard to make more money to buy more things. As a result, these people end up with little time to enjoy life.

Remember that money isn't everything. It may give you a feeling of superiority or success. However, when you get down to the bottom line of meeting and dealing with people, it is you who will make the final impression. Your personality, your values, and your ability to respect yourself as a person will lead others to their final judgments about you.

If you can give money a realistic and proper place as your priorities develop, you will be a much happier and more contented adult. Your high school years and your enjoyment of them will be much richer, too.

Points to Ponder

1. Do you feel you have a realistic attitude toward money? How important is money to you? Be specific.

_____

_____

_____

2. How would you advise a friend who is tempted to steal?

_____

_____

_____

3. How well do you understand your family's financial position, and how clearly do you accept those limits?

_____

_____

_____

4. How many hours a week do you think a high school student should work at a job? How would you make time for a job right now?

_____

_____

5. How much money do you feel you need each month? Make a budget to show where the money will be going.

_____

_____

_____

Pressures, Problems, and Possibilities

15

The bad news is that, no matter how much advice you get on how things should go during your high school years, there are still many problems you will have to face. The good news, though, is that the way you face any pressure or problem says a lot about you as a person. It shows how strong you have become since you entered your teens, and whether you are still a "kid."

There are those who say people never know their true character until a difficult situation arises. That's when we find out what we're made of. Let's make an attempt to find out what you are made of.

Where Do You Stand?

In the spaces that follow, write an answer about how you think you might react to the situation described. Be as honest as you can.

1. Your friend is thinking of committing suicide. You see many of the signs, and you fear this may not be just an act. What would you do?

_____

_____

2. Some people you know decide to make your life miserable by putting you down and telling lies behind your back. What is your reaction?

_____

_____

3. You feel your friends are, more and more, making you do things you really don't want to do. What do you do?

_____

_____

4. On a scale of 1 to 10, with 10 being the highest, rate your personality. Describe your strong points and your weaknesses.

_____

_____

_____

_____

_____

_____

5. What do you feel will be the two biggest problems for you as the new century unfolds?

_____

_____

_____

6. What two things could you do to increase your ability to deal with these and other problems?

_____

_____

_____

7. What are two pressures you feel you need to do something to alleviate within the next two years, and how can you try to do that?

_____

_____

_____

You May Be Your Biggest Problem

Your attitude toward yourself may be the cause of some of your most difficult problems. If this is so, it *is* possible to improve the situation.

First, consider your body. You may feel no one would especially want to do that, and you may be right. Are you concerned about your weight or about some physical feature you feel may be keeping others away from you? If so, something in your attitude toward others may be letting people know you are unhappy about yourself.

If some feature about your body makes you insecure, it may make you louder than you should be. You may feel you have to be more fun to be with, so people will like you. You may go to the other extreme and retreat into a shell in an attempt to shut yourself off from any possibility of rejection.

You are at a time of life when you may be overly concerned about your looks and your body. If not checked, this concern could turn into a big problem for you.

Learn to Accept, Except . . .

No one goes through life these days without being bombarded with pictures from TV, movies, or other forms of the media that give you some false ideas about how you should look. You may have fallen into the trap of thinking that all teens should look like the fresh, blond actors who advertise everything from acne medications to toothpaste, or who look so terrific in videos and movies. The cable and network sitcoms have many good-looking guys and girls who are not only making a lot of money but are the envy of many people their own age. But these actors are just that—actors. Tons of money and makeup go into making them look the way they do.

Try watching the news instead of the films or commercials. On the news, you will see real-world people being interviewed. You will then start to realize that the people you see on the screens are idealized, not real.

Learning to feel comfortable with your body and your looks means accepting what you cannot change, and honestly trying to do something about those things you can control. Braces, acne, and some baby fat may be part of the territory right now, but they are not permanent. A good look at acne medicines or a trip to a dermatologist may at least get acne under control. Braces have become so common that they are hardly even noticed. If you let them be a problem for you, you are just not noticing that half of your classmates have them, too. Just think of that million-dollar smile you'll have some day! Likewise, you may feel your body is not maturing as quickly as those of your friends or the other guys or girls in the locker room. Try to remember that people develop at their own pace. Your adult body will take its true form soon enough.

You may not like your nose, your eyes, or your ears. You may detest the fact you inherited the family chin. You may be miserable about the curl, or lack of it, in your hair. But these are the features that make you who you are. As soon as you begin to accept them as part of your own unique-ness, and sometimes part of your wonderful ethnic heritage, you can begin to feel comfortable about yourself. You are not a carbon copy of a television commercial, and that is what is so terrific about you! You are an individual, and you look like an individual.

Leave the house each morning looking your best. If you are clean and put together as well as you can be, relax and enjoy yourself. If others cannot accept how you look, that is their problem. It is not yours.

It's All in My Mind

Another problem you may face during your teens is the fear that you are not smart enough. With the pressure for getting good grades stronger than ever, you may feel you cannot cope. You may fear getting low scores on the SATs or other standardized tests—tools that have come to mean so much when it comes to college acceptance.

A talk with your counselor will help. You have a legal right to see the results of IQ tests and scholastic achieve-ment scores, as well as your school file. Ask your counselor to help you evaluate and understand your scores. In this way, you can get a realistic idea of your abilities and possible weaknesses. You can begin to put forth more effort in areas where you need it, and start to be more comfort-able with your own level of intelligence. You can also begin to use your scores to discover various aptitudes and career choices for which you're well-suited.

Just remember that as the body matures at different levels in different people, so does the mind. You may not have had the challenge or the ambition to use all your brainpower up to this point. That is no indication that you will not use it in the future. With technology making advances as the century moves on, and new challenges appearing every day, you may be one of the pioneers in a field that hasn't even been invented yet.

Never give up on yourself. Never give up on your ability. You have no idea at your young age what greatness you can achieve through the rest of your life.

Personality—Plus or Total Zero?

If someone asked you to draw a picture of your personality, would you produce a blank piece of paper? Guess what? You're not alone. Many people are not totally happy with their personalities. Most don't even understand what personality really is.

Your personality comes from the essential *you*, the person you began to discover in the first few chapters of this book. The way you react, either as a thinker, a doer, a leader, or a producer will determine your personality. As an extrovert, you may feel comfortable taking charge of situations and conversations. You may feel more secure in a group. If you are a more thoughtful type, you may choose to sit back and let others take the initiative while you get a better view of the situation. You may need time alone once in a while just to sort things out. That's fine, as long as the time alone doesn't claim more and more of your life. That could be a danger sign.

In whatever way you react, your basic personality must be geared toward others. The different ways you communicate with them and respond to them will give them their only clues to your real identity. If you can honestly be yourself, your personality will evolve very naturally and comfortably for you and the people you meet. In some writing classes, students often express a desire to develop a writing style. Any good teacher will give the best advice: the more the writer develops as a person, the more his or her writing style will develop, since writing is simply putting yourself and your thoughts on paper.

No one is happy all the time, but it is not normal to always be miserable, either. Your moods will swing back and forth; that's only human. The secret lies in not letting one mood grab hold of you and stay too long. Sickness, sadness, and even death will come into your life as you care for the people you love. Feeling periods of sadness, or mourning those who have died, is very human, and an act of love for them.

But refusing to put the past into perspective can be the beginning of real psychological problems. If you can stay open to yourself and others and keep a positive attitude, you can soon get on top of any mood and let the normal happiness of life take over again. Even mourning ends, and eventually a new morning dawns inside you.

Do you want a good personality? Just be the you that makes you feel most comfortable, sincere, and human. The honest person is a breath of fresh air in our society. Be one, and let others share that open, sunny feeling when they meet you.

Pressure Is a Pain!

Too much pressure certainly is a pain. But whether you like it or not, high school life involves all kinds of pressure. The secret to dealing with pressure is in learning how to cope with it and learning how to relieve it.

Experts say one of the chief causes of illness and depression in people of all ages is the pressures of modern life. With more and more activities now crammed into the same time, and more demands put on individuals to succeed in their careers and still have time for family and personal development, the ability to handle pressure will be key to you not only now but throughout your life. Is handling such pressures possible? Absolutely!

School pressures may come in the guise of big exams, which are enough to put many in a state of panic. How do you handle them? You can tell everyone about them, complain about them, and let everyone know that you're worried, but often this just reinforces your feelings of tension.

Another approach involves taking a hard look at why tests have you in such a state. The best strategy is to prepare for each test as best you can, and go to it presuming you will do your best. Arrange a work session with others so you can compare notes. Go over the material for each test the night before, right before you go to bed. It has been proven that the mind works while we sleep, so by reviewing material right before you fall asleep, it may be easier for you to recall it when you need it during a test the next day.

Understanding and dealing with sources of pressure is a way of succeeding in much more than high school. If you can learn to handle stress during your teens, your adult life will be a lot more pleasant. You will also save a lot of money on doctor bills.

Peer Pressure

Perhaps the strongest pressure you feel in your teen years is peer pressure. You are not alone in your desire to be accepted, liked, and thought of as successful. All people want to be liked, to have friends, and to win the affection and respect of others.

During high school, however, when young people are still trying to understand themselves, popularity seems to be especially important. Teens need to feel they are competing successfully for others' attention. With the close atmosphere of family receding and lifelong relationships of their own still in the future, young people need to belong to some group and know there is a special place where they are accepted.

The secret in handling peer pressure lies in understanding yourself and respecting your individuality. Many teens boast they are independent while actually being some of the biggest followers around. They wear only what's in style; they listen only to "acceptable" music, and they only express attitudes other teens consider correct.

That's not individuality. That's caving in to peer pressure.

You will be expected to concede on occasion to please friends. Life is a give-and-take affair. Also, there will be times when you may decide to do what others want because you want to be nice to them. The bottom line in dealing with peer pressure, though, is this: promise yourself never to sell out on what is important to you.

Please Yourself

If your friends continually ask you to go against your own convictions, or pressure you into choices that aren't comfortable for you, perhaps you and your "friends" are growing in two different directions. You may need to take another look at the people in your life, especially the people you want to be like.

Peer pressure in no simple problem. No teen wants to be left out of the action or feel forced to spend evening after evening at home because he or she cannot make friends. The secret is in learning how to choose friends wisely in the first place and then remaining true to yourself while you are with them. If this happens, your friends will know and respect you. They will usually recognize your individuality rather than make you follow their lead.

High school is a time for learning, and one of the biggest lessons you can learn before that diploma is tucked under your arm is a solid faith in your own worth as a person. Peer pressure does not stop in adult life. It may become more subtle, but it is always there. If you can learn how to handle it and remain true to your good friends and your own convictions at the same time, you will be several giant steps ahead of many people.

Are You an Addict?

Having reached high school age, you have probably already been invited or involved in "partying" with a group of people. What the term "partying" means, however, has many interpretations. Depending on where you live, it may mean getting together to drink alcohol, or it may involve using marijuana and other drugs.

The problem of alcohol and drugs in our society cannot be underestimated, and it is a growing concern for people of your age. You may already be fighting your own battles with them. If you can begin winning those battles, you are making a big step toward adulthood. There are many teens now who have already made mistakes and are fighting their way out from under the spell of drugs and moving on into productive lives. If you need to fight, fight. If you still have the chance, make the decision not to become an addict in the first place.

The Bottom Line

The secret to dealing with pressure to use drugs is to be your own person in any situation. If your insecurity prevents you from forming strong convictions of your own, it won't be easy to refuse that joint or pill, or to decide you would rather not get drunk. You will go along with the crowd.

Only you can choose which way to go. Remember that artificial means of being happy are only temporary escapes from reality. Hiding under a cloud of smoke does not make your problems go away.

The decision about whether to use alcohol or other drugs is one of the roughest you will make during high school. It will also affect your later life considerably. Make that decision carefully. You owe that much to yourself and to the people who love you.

Sex, Dating, and Peer Pressure

Dating can bring on another tremendous pressure. Magazine ads, websites, and music all remind us that we are living in a sex-conscious society. The macho image is prevalent in all commercials aimed at men. The sexy, appealing woman stares at us from ads selling things as ordinary as toothpaste.

This emphasis on sex becomes evident to teens when a couple begins to start feeling pressure to live up to a certain image. Boys sometimes feel they must have something suggestive or racy to say in the locker room on Monday. Girls often feel they have to go along with a guy's request on a date or never have a date again. The pressure is tremendous.

This is another form of peer pressure, and it can be handled in the same way. Whether you are a boy or a girl, your date may tell others that things happened when they didn't. However, you and your partner know what really happened, and you must learn to be comfortable with that knowledge. There are few things in life you *must* do. Freedom is the one thing every individual holds sacred. Our country was founded on an intense belief in it. Never let someone or some pressure for acceptance get in the way of your personal freedom and right to make your own choices.

Make your life what you want it to be. Choose to be who you want to be. Do yourself a favor. Base your decisions on a solid respect for yourself and your own personal integrity. The people who are important to you will understand. The others, by failing to accept the fact that you live your own life, will prove they never really deserved your friendship in the first place.

Make Sure There Is a Future—the Reality of Suicide

For some, thinking about the future and dealing with the stress of being a teen can become overwhelming. Suicide is one of the greatest causes of teen death today. It's a tough subject, but it's one you must face, if not for yourself, then for friends or other people you know. While you may have sense enough to realize that suicide never solves anything, at some point you may need to help someone else who is struggling with this issue.

Why would a teen consider suicide? Some would say it goes back to the "raps" we will talk about in chapter 17—that all teens want is entertainment, that they cannot face life's hard realities. Most people understand, though, that teens who attempt suicide are troubled and feeling hopeless.

Whatever the cause, too many teens decide that suicide is the only way out of their problems. Some go through the motions just to get someone's attention, wrongly believing they won't really die. Others really want to commit suicide.

The trouble is, suicide is a permanent solution to very temporary problems. No pain or hurt is permanent. Only death is permanent. It is horribly painful to anyone who has cared about or loved that person, as well.

If you ever consider committing suicide because you see no end to your problems or misery, stop a minute. Can you really believe there is no one and no group of people who will eventually care about you and truly love you? If you answer yes, you are wrong. No one knows what the future holds. Believe that even the worst conditions will end on their own. They do. Life moves on. People and situations change. You will change, too. Don't let yourself—or anyone you know—fall into the trap of ending temporary pain with such an extreme act. Instead, seek help and give yourself the future you deserve, and the future others truly want for you.

If you see friends giving away possessions, talking of suicide, or changing their lifestyle and habits, talk to a counselor, a teacher, or other trusted adult. See anyone who can help. Don't wait. Be the caring friend who can convince a possible suicide that there *are* people who care and who do not want their friends to die.

Rapping It Up

Problems are an unavoidable part of our lives. The secret to dealing with them is to face them honestly and understand what they are doing to us. Hiding from problems or trying to escape from them only brings on a whole new set of problems—sometimes more serious ones.

Your ability to handle difficult situations comes from your own concept of yourself. If you know who you are and what you want, you can put each difficulty into perspective. You can make intelligent choices.

All people have problems. The truly great people, however, have learned how to cut their problems down to size by facing them squarely and taking action to solve them. How well you succeed in high school will be determined by who wins the battle—your problems or you. You can win that battle by using the ultimate secret weapon—yourself!

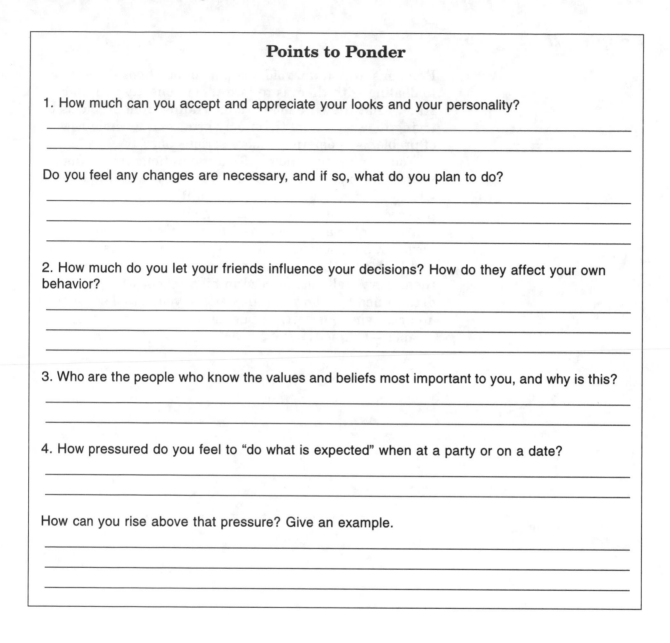

Points to Ponder

1. How much can you accept and appreciate your looks and your personality?

_____

_____

Do you feel any changes are necessary, and if so, what do you plan to do?

_____

_____

_____

2. How much do you let your friends influence your decisions? How do they affect your own behavior?

_____

_____

_____

3. Who are the people who know the values and beliefs most important to you, and why is this?

_____

_____

4. How pressured do you feel to "do what is expected" when at a party or on a date?

_____

_____

How can you rise above that pressure? Give an example.

_____

_____

_____

Coping with Crisis

16

"I've never made a mistake in my life, except once, when I thought I had made one."

That's an old joke, and the humor of it lies in the fact that everyone does make mistakes. To think otherwise is foolish. But then, there are *your* mistakes! "Somehow everyone doesn't see my mistakes as a joke," you might say. "It seems I'm always doing something wrong. At least, that's what people tell me!"

Others may tell you, sometimes in anger or disappointment, that you have failed. But even worse is that sick, horrible feeling when you realize you've really "messed up," as the saying goes. It is miserable to know you've disappointed someone or acted poorly when something really counted. No one can forget that frustrating feeling, that emptiness and anger at yourself. It hurts, knowing you may have hurt others.

Mistakes, the feeling of failure, and the depression that is sure to come are hard to take. While you're in your teens, these feelings can be even more devastating. You're at a stage of life when report cards keep reminding you of your success or lack of it. Every grading period at school you see a computer printout of where you may have failed. After a few mistakes on your part, you naturally become a bit more cautious. You pull back. You may even start to feel suspicious, fearful, and on the lookout for the next time someone will catch you doing wrong. Soon you may begin to feel the tension of always being on the defensive.

It is that fear of doing wrong, in fact, that often keeps many people from trying at all. After you've experienced a few colossal failures, you may be tempted to play it safe, do as little as possible, and stay at least partially successful. However, the fact remains that the only people who never do anything wrong are the people who never do anything!

Everyone Does It

The first thing to remember whenever you get that sick feeling of failure is that you are not alone. Failure is part of life. How you handle it will determine whether you're able to learn from your errors and move on with your life. You're going to make mistakes, but the true test is whether failure destroys your self-confidence or makes you more determined to change things for the better.

Recall the things you've learned so far about your own personality. How positive can you be? How excited can you get about the possibility of things improving? How fast can you bounce back from hard times? How do you deal with failure? Do you blame others? Do you keep it all inside and give yourself forty mental lashes, or do you share it with someone, clearing the air and putting it behind you?

The next time you fail, look at what happened. Where did the failure occur, and how much was directly your responsibility? Was it someone else's rejection that made you feel like a failure? Was it a failed test, not being chosen for a team or a part in a play, or breaking a rule at home or at school?

The Biggest Disappointment

One of Beth's dearest friends told her a confidential secret. The friend had gotten into a serious situation and wanted it kept private. To ease her anxiety, though, she shared the problem with Beth. Beth knew it was serious and could hurt her friend's reputation if word got around. However, at lunch one day Beth put her mouth into operation before her brain was in gear. She let part of the secret slip out.

Once she said the words, Beth knew she had betrayed a confidence, and a horrible feeling came over her. When the others asked for more information, she knew she had already said too much, and she tried to back down on the story. But she had said enough, and the damage was done.

That feeling of knowing you failed miserably when someone trusted you can be shattering. You know you're a better person than that. You know you can be trusted and that you care. You know it—but at times you also know you can lose it all and fail as a friend. What can you do?

It happens. Face up to your mistake, and then see what you have learned. This may sound a bit strange, but sometimes the best way to learn is by getting things wrong. Missing a question on a quiz may make you remember that information more clearly than if you had gotten it right the first time. That little feeling of anger at yourself makes a strong impression on your mind. The next time you see that question, it will be much easier to answer.

Now that Beth has betrayed her friend, she has a few choices. She can lie about it and say someone else must have leaked the news. She can be cold, saying the other girl is expecting too much, and defend herself. But the best thing, and the only honest thing, is to let her friend know she told the secret (without meaning to), and that she is sorry. Few personal failures are intentional. Beth didn't want to hurt her friend. It just happened.

Once she admitted this to herself, she began to think twice before speaking about secrets she knew. You can learn the same kind of lesson.

Making the Same Mistake Twice

You may not learn from a mistake the first time you make it. If we all learned from our mistakes as they happened, we would reach perfection around age twenty-five or twenty-six. You may have realized by watching some adults that this isn't the case! You may do something wrong and, weeks or months later, make the same mistake again.

This, too proves you are just human. When you repeat a mistake, go back and check your list of values and priorities. If something is important to you, you probably will learn it the first time and move on. If it isn't important, that impression won't be as strong. When the temptation presents itself again, you may fail again.

You will have to determine what is important. Do you want to be a good friend? Do you want others to think of you as someone they can trust? If you answer yes, you'll learn how to keep your friends' confidences. You are responsible when it comes to your failings, just as you are responsible for every other part of your life. If you can learn that one mistake isn't going to ruin you, you'll be all right. It's keeping the right intention in your heart and in your attitudes toward friends and life that will put you in the mindset necessary for being a loyal and good friend.

People Problems

You can't control other people. You can't always please them, and you definitely can't always be aware of how they will react to you or your decisions.

Rejection, for example, is one of the hardest things. You may want someone, or some group, to accept you. You do your best. You really try, and still you are rejected. They just don't seem to want you, and that hurts. What can you do?

You can look at possible reasons. There may be a flaw in your personality, and there may not be. Those others may just not be your kind of people. They may be too busy in their own worlds to discover how interesting and pleasant it is to be with you. That's their problem. It may hurt for a while, but don't let it be your problem.

When you fail with people who are already a part of your life, you'll have to learn some hard facts, too. Your parents, for example, will let you know when you've let them down. They may even tell you how disappointed they are, and that can really get to you.

Consider this girl's situation: "I remember one night, after we had a horrible fight. I was really angry, and I said a lot of things I probably didn't mean. But I was mad, and I wanted my parents to know it. Later, I walked into the kitchen and saw my mother sitting at the table, her head in her hands. She was crying. She just looked at me, and I wanted to die! I do love her, but she had made me so mad. I felt so confused and so mad. I was mad at myself for hurting her and still mad at her for what she had done. Talk about confusion!"

When you hurt the people you love, it is not easy to get over the experience. You can try to understand it later, when you are in a calmer state of mind. Often that will be the best thing to do. Just remembering how you felt is the first step. In this girl's case, those tears in her mother's eyes taught a greater lesson than any lecture, sermon, or book.

Parents and Teachers

There will be times when family members and teachers can make you feel bad. A parent going through a divorce can often try to turn children against the marriage partner who is leaving. This not only tears up everyone's feelings; it can also make the sons and daughters feel terribly guilty. Some parents make their children feel guilty every time they do wrong. "I really am a rotten parent," they'll say. "I tried so hard, and now you act like this. Where did I go wrong?" Feeling like a failure usually includes a feeling of guilt. You get enough of it on your own; you don't need any more. If your folks have the habit of making you feel guilty, try talking to them about it. Don't let yourself feel guilty all the time. There's no future in it.

Family conflict is always rough. When someone outside the home says you have failed, you can at least go home and forget it. When the people you live with do it, you'll have to get some honest communication going or the problem will only get worse.

Teachers may also make you feel you have failed. A poor grade on a report card or a critical teacher conference are also hard to face. However, most often these feelings can be eased by speaking frankly about yourself. If you can get the teacher to see you as a person with individual needs, frustrations, and dreams, he or she will listen. That doesn't mean that your test scores won't affect your grade. But if the teacher understands a bit more about you, he or she may make more of an effort to help you do well in the course.

What's the best way to deal with your failures with others? Talk to them. Explain your point of view without being defensive. Listen without judging. Usually, once you discuss emotional differences, a lot more understanding will flow between you and other people. From there, the road to success will have fewer bumps. Once again, communication is the key.

Forget the Labels

Never label yourself a failure. So, you didn't get an A on that last test, and you didn't make the team, the first chair in band, or the play. Maybe your story wasn't chosen as one of the best in the class, and you don't seem to do anything well enough to please your math teacher. True, you may not be a genius, and you may have two left feet. But everyone around you has their weaknesses, too.

Failing at one thing doesn't mean you are a failure. Most people who let their failures affect them are individuals who can't work up the courage to try again. Do try! Find the things you're good at, and move on. You may find a clue to your true talents in some item announced in the next school bulletin, or hidden in a conversation you'll soon have with a friend. Your abilities are there, just begging for you to discover them. Give it a try!

Rapping It Up

Failure is something that occasionally appears in your life. What can you do about it?

You can learn not to fear it, and you can begin to make failure work for you, not against you. By letting it sink in, understanding the reason for it, and then deciding to go on, you can ensure that failures don't ruin your life or keep you from an honest and true pursuit of your dreams.

There is no shame in failing, and there is no shame in admitting it. In fact, it may be one of the healthiest things you can do. The only shame lies in wallowing in your own defeat and deciding not to go on. The only person who fails is the person who has given up. If you can keep loving yourself, the people around you, and the things that are important to you, you're bound to succeed eventually.

Points to Ponder

1. What kinds of failure do you fear most, and why?

_____

_____

_____

2. Which of your personality traits cause most of your failures? Explain with an example.

_____

_____

_____

_____

3. How often do you let feelings of guilt linger?

_____

What do you do to get rid of them?

_____

_____

4. Give an example of one instance when you learned from a mistake. Be specific.

_____

_____

_____

_____

5. What advice would you give a friend who feels there is no use in trying again after a rejection or a failure?

_____

_____

_____

_____

Beating the Raps

17

Guaranteed. The hardest chapter to read in this book.

Guaranteed. Some words to make you think, and possibly make you angry.

Guaranteed. Some of the best words you can read at this time in your life.

No book on succeeding in high school would be fair to you, or complete, without letting you know what others think of your generation. While adults have something to say about every teen generation, something different seems to be happening lately.

Many people, from teachers and businesspeople to parents and psychologists, all agree that something has been happening to young people, and whatever it is, the adult community is very worried about it.

We're talking about a rap here, not in the style of rap music, but in the sense of harsh blame. Why are these adults so concerned?

In the next few pages, we'll go over some of the biggest raps. You may find yourself in them, or you may be angry about them because they aren't true in your case. In any case, here are the problems people see in your age group these days. Read them, and if they ring true, determine to make some changes so they don't apply to you and your future.

"They Just Don't Care"

Teens are so busy sorting out their own lives that many of them don't have time to get too involved in keeping up with world events. That has always been the case. But some people feel that teens today show an attitude that goes even further. Many in your age group not only don't know, but don't seem to care that they don't know. That's a big difference. You may know the bigger things. You may know that America impeached a president, with all the press coverage that involved, and that when you were a child, there was a short war in the Persian Gulf.

But do you form your own opinions about world events? Do you take time to analyze them and stay informed about them? An important step in growing up is learning to care about things outside yourself. Being a mature adult means giving up the self-absorption that's natural in children. As an adult, you are not only a responsible member of your own family but an important member of your community and the world. With any destination within a few clicks away on your computer, you can now be in touch with anyone, anywhere. You have instant access to the richness of the world's cultures.

How can you respond? Try to keep your mind open to new ideas and opinions, and don't let other people make your opinions for you. Read a newspaper or watch some news once in a while. Turn off the music channel long enough to learn what's going on in the world. Let yourself be open to events and concerns the world is sharing, and when you're old enough, register to vote.

Another step is to *want* to learn, rather than viewing it as something that is inflicted on you merely because of your age and society's laws. Education is a privilege of free societies. Value yours.

"They're So Selfish!"

The second big rap involves a feeling that people in your age group don't care about anything except your own pleasure. If it isn't "fun" for you, you don't want any part of it. You seem to be very materialistic, expecting rewards for everything you do, even if your work and effort are only mediocre. From expecting to be paid for good report cards to demanding good grades at school or more spending money on the home front, many teens are creating the impression they are only interested in taking.

How can you respond to these charges? Prove people wrong by your actions. When needs arise in your school, community, or family, show your concern. See where you can help. Get in the giving mode. And develop a personal code of ethics that shows a healthy respect for others as well as for yourself.

"They Have No Motivation"

Many adults feel most teens have no real motivation and no follow-through on projects. "It's as if the last burner isn't on with these kids," some say. "They seem to be in some kind of fog, and they don't mind being in it. They can't be counted on to follow through on projects, and they don't place any value on membership in anything—from a family to a team or a group."

Those who sponsor extracurricular activities at schools echo this sentiment. From the teacher who has to take over preparations for a fund-raiser to another who has to finish the work her staff members or theater group didn't get done, many feel this is the wrong time to be involved with activities where student participation is involved. They say, "Students start out and talk about their plans a long time. But then they fall behind far from the finish line, or they do work that is so poor it can't be used."

If you think there's a teacher or coach who feels this way about you, what should you do? In the words of one coach, "Get with it!" Show adults in your life you can be responsible, and follow through on things that are on your plate. Prove that you do have a desire to make things happen. Get involved not for the glory or for another picture in the yearbook, but because you have something to give to these groups. Give to them, and they will give back to you in many ways.

"They Don't Want to Work"

The third rap is a charge of laziness and acceptance of mediocrity. Many local employers feel teens aren't worth hiring because they do the least work and then expect pay much higher than they deserve. The big rap is that teens tend to accept mediocrity as the norm and that they have little desire to give solid effort to any project. Self-esteem comes from knowing you gave your best to a project, and that you tried at whatever task you were given. You'll know when you've done well, and then you won't have to worry about having any self-esteem. You'll be too busy moving on to other things.

Some schools have watered down their grading systems; yours may be one of them. When your parents went to school in the Dark Ages, 70 percent was a passing grade, and 69 percent was a failure. Students had to achieve 95 percent or higher to get an A. In some schools now, grading levels have been lowered, with anything higher than 90 percent called an A.

Yet when teachers give percentage grades or letter grades, many feel students demand higher marks for mediocre work. "It's as if we've lowered all our standards and norms for real excellence," one teacher said recently. "Students do half-baked work and then are angry when they don't get the highest grades."

You may need to realize that merely doing a project is only half the battle. Doing it well is the other half. Writing a paper and handing in the first draft is not usually worth a good grade. If this is your mode of operation, don't expect the highest mark for mediocre effort. Most papers need some revision before they're considered a writer's best.

How can you beat this rap? Work. It's okay to take time to relax and enjoy your friends or listen to music. But when work needs to be done, do it. Remember that section on work ethic in Chapter 6? Review it if you need to. Show people you know how to make an honest effort, that you understand commitment to a job and a desire to do something worthwhile.

Don't be like the teenager who sat listening to his earphones while his mother raked all the leaves in the yard, then told his neighbor she'd better get working on her own yard. Let others know you are willing to adopt the work ethic that has built this country. Let adults know you're willing to add your own effort in making it even better.

"They Hate Too Much and Think Too Little"

Because of teens' tendency to follow the crowd, which often leads to heavy drinking, drugs, and other things, adults also say teens are a bunch of sheep. Whether it's belonging to a gang or hanging out with a clique, many teens seem to give in to herd mentality thinking.

You've been accused of having little creativity and independence. You've been accused of being used by everyone from drug dealers to some of your own pseudo-intellectual leaders. Too many in your age group have in fact learned to hate. Hate groups target teenagers who are searching for a place to belong and something to believe in.

Hatred and racism do nothing but burn up the people who hate. Cruelty and hatred against another human being are unacceptable. Neither makes it in the workplace or elsewhere in the adult world. And neither will you, as long as you hate and exhibit violence or cruel tendencies.

Most adults hope we're moving beyond the hatred of earlier times. To see young people take up the banner of hatred again is to feel that the world is not improving, and worse, that we're possibly regressing to earlier mistakes. Adults want to look to you for hope for better things ahead. Give them reason to hope.

"They Can't Accept Responsibility"

Another rap you can really do something about is the belief you can't accept responsibility for your actions or words. Parents, teachers, and employers are quick to give examples of teens' inability to take responsibility or blame for anything. "The student blamed me for his bad grade. Yet it was his low test scores that added up to that final mark. His answer is that I don't like him. That's why he got the low grade."

One parent said, "My daughter can never admit she did anything wrong. It's always someone else's fault. She's so quick to defend herself; she seems unable to admit she can make mistakes. Halfway through any sentence when I'm telling her what went wrong, she's already interrupting with an excuse that puts all the blame on someone or something else! Why can't she realize that some things are her fault?"

What's the answer? Easy. No one expects you to be perfect. No one expects you to be right all the time and never make mistakes. No one expects you to achieve your best all the time. We all have bad days. Just admit it when you do have them. Admit you didn't handle a project or situation well. Admit you made a mistake. It's the adult thing to do.

Rapping It Up

By this time, you may be ready to burn this book. Instead, give it to someone else to read, and start a new fire inside yourself. Now that you know what some adults think about your age group these days, be determined to show that you don't fit any of these negative descriptions.

Care about the world around you and the world in which you live. Care about your family members and friends, because they're going through their own changes and struggles. Care about your ability to live responsibly and productively in the adult world. Don't be afraid to go out of your way to show concern for others. Try to show your desire to know what the world is thinking and feeling. Get into the giving mode.

If you want the respect of others and expect them to begin treating you like an adult, start accepting and acknowledging responsibility. Listen to others' criticism of your work, then consider their words and make a reasonable response. It is childish to always puts the blame elsewhere. Constantly fighting off blame doesn't give others the idea that you have moved much beyond childhood.

Show some motivation at home, in school, in the community, and in your life. Finish the projects you start, and decide to make a valid contribution to the groups in which you hold membership. Rather than expect favors or fight about grades, produce. Show others you're not afraid of hard work and that you have the ability to see things through with the best effort you can give.

So much for the raps. Now the world awaits your response.

Points to Ponder

1. Name something you could do this week to become better informed about current events.

_____

_____

2. What was the last generous thing you did for someone in your family? Name something else you could do to show your parents or brothers and sisters that you care.

_____

_____

_____

3. Are you in the middle of any extracurricular or class projects? How do you plan to complete them on time and with as much quality as possible?

_____

_____

_____

4. How strong would you rate your work ethic, with ten being the highest? What could you do to improve your work at home, in school, or at your part-time job?

_____

_____

_____

5. How much do others influence your opinions and actions? Explain and give an example.

_____

_____

_____

_____

6. Are you able to admit when you've made a mistake? Explain with an example.

_____

_____

_____

_____

Guidelines for a New Century

18

High school remains high school. But as the new century begins, there are some subtle changes that have occurred in the adult world that can affect teens even while they're still in high school.

It's About Time

One thing people in the working world have learned, and which many teens are already starting to cope with, is that time is of the essence in this new era. In these hectic times, time management has become an art as pressures and demands mount up.

There are many day planners and calendars available at discount stationery stores, and many of them are specially geared to the school year, starting at September and going through June. You may be aware that some of your classmates are already using calendars.

Investing in a good daily, weekly, or monthly planner is one way of keeping ahead of all the demands on your time, which include everything from daily homework, time for long-term projects, time at home, time with friends, get-togethers, and all the various things that will quickly crowd up your calendar as time moves on.

Getting in the habit of keeping a day or month planner is a good thing. It will give you an idea of your obligations and responsibilities at a glance, and also help you get the feeling you are in control of your life, not just a person who has to keep juggling time.

As you fill in some of those days and evenings, don't let obligations be the only entries. Between home, part-time jobs, family, and friends, make sure you even block out some time for yourself periodically. You will only be effective with other people as you are aware of yourself and your own priorities. Time set aside for yourself to get things in order, or just quiet time for you to use as you wish, is very important. The demands of the outside world are never going to lessen, and when you get a full-time job later on, pressures from all sides will only increase. Learning to use your time wisely now, and setting blocks of time aside for the important things in your life, will be a lifelong skill you can use.

You may have grown up running from school to dance or music lessons, to practice for some sport or activity, and with little time to stop, relax, and simply find out who you really are. As you move through high school, you now have the opportunity to be more selective about what activities you choose, and how much time you need for yourself. Your parents wanted to give you many opportunities when you were a child, and if you had those opportunities, be glad. But now you are working on becoming your own person. You can choose what you will get involved in, and be comfortable with your choices.

A Little Help from Friends

While The Beatles may be part of the old Stone Age to you, they certainly have become classics, and when you take the time to review some of their more memorable music, you'll find a simple song in the *Sergeant Pepper* CD that states, "I get by with a little help from my friends."

Very true. While we've talked in other parts of this book about false friends and the search for friends, the truth remains that when you find good friends in your life, they can become more precious than gold. A classic definition of a good friend is someone who really knows you—and still likes you! When you develop a few friends like that, it is very important to hang on to them, because as the pressures of life crowd in around you, it is those friends who will be your rock. Good friends are the glue that can often mean the difference between feeling lonely and even alienated and a more easy way of handling pressures. They are there when we need them, and they are there when we need to let off steam or confide some of our deepest feelings.

As you get busy, don't forget to take care of those friendships. Friendship is always a two-way street that demands giving as well as taking. When you have found a good friend, think long and hard before you let anything destroy that very special kind of bond.

Be There

One of the most common problems facing high schools, colleges, and even the work world these days is absenteeism. High school teachers complain that some teens feel free to take a day off whenever they think they feel the need. If attendance doesn't seem like a big thing to you, remember that being there is always half of the battle. Showing up for class, social functions, and meetings is one of the basic elements of success. Attending school now, and being on time, is a habit that will carry over into the work world when you are expected to be at a job at a certain time.

The success of your business right now is passing your classes and getting all you can from the high school experience. If you put yourself at a disadvantage by often putting yourself in the position of having to catch up, or make up work, you deprive yourself of a fair chance at success.

If you need more sleep, get more sleep. If you need five alarm clocks in the morning, then use them. Don't fall into the trap of thinking the world owes you a day off periodically just because you feel the need for it. People like that are the first to be fired from jobs, and they are the first who lose the interest of teachers and administrators who normally would want to help and give the benefit of the doubt when problems arise.

Stress Need Not Be Distress

One of the biggest topics of concern these days is the amount of stress in people's lives. Stress affects not only the quality of life, but physical and mental health as well. One of the things you'll need to learn is that stress in some form is normal and doesn't need to cause you drastic concern. Society has a way of putting us into roles, and then expecting us to deal with the pressures of those roles. There's nothing wrong about that.

The only problem with stress is when it gets to be too much, it causes distress in your life. When the pressure gets too great and you get the feeling you're trapped in something you can't escape, that's distress. The human psyche has built-in safeguards to handle stress, but when you may feel that you can't cope, you may be blocking some of those safeguards. That's when the temptation to find an escape comes in, and that's why some people turn to things that give temporary escape, but in reality only add greater pressures. Trying to escape stress is not the answer. Rather, learn how to find the sources of stress and then take care of them one at a time. For instance, you might want to cut out some of your weekly activities, or speak with a counselor for other ideas.

Rapping It Up

Your place in this new century is assured, as long as you can hold on to a strong belief in yourself and in your abilities to cope with whatever is ahead of all of us. You live in a time of change in your own life, moving ever closer to your own adult life. You also live in a time of tremendous change in society and the world. Your willingness to take on the burdens of your life right now, complete with school, family, and outside involvement, will give you a great possibility of success.

Take some time to study time and how it works in your life. Don't be its slave, but rather be a master of time.

Learning to use a planner or calendar system will give you the feeling you are in control, and that is half the battle.

Learn to respect and value good friends. These are not the people who give you a better image at school, or who pay your way to things because they have more money in their pocket. These are the honest people who really know you and still like you. They can help you endure some of the darkest times, and they can keep giving you perspective on your life, your attitudes, and the reality of your goals.

Don't be afraid of stress. Consider it as just another hurdle to leap over on your way to success. Learn to identify its sources. Some of the stressors will come from outside you, and you will have to learn to deal with them. The stresses you put on yourself are usually the most damaging, and you can handle them by taking time to understand why you give them so much power over you.

At a time in your life when you feel you may still be too young to be taken seriously by some people, consider the fact you are older than this new century. This is a time when youth and new ideas are more needed than ever. People are ready for change, and society will be waiting for you when you decide you are ready to make your mark on the world.

Points to Ponder

1. What items would you put in a calendar or day planning system, and how would that help your ability to handle all of time's pressures on you?

_____

_____

_____

_____

2. How would you describe the value you put on good friends?

_____

_____

_____

3. What are three big sources of stress in your life right now, and what specific things can you do to bring them under control?

_____

_____

_____

_____

4. What are some of the biggest goals you set for yourself by the time you are twenty-five, thirty-five, and fifty-five?

_____

_____

_____

_____

Free at Last

19

Every country values it. Many nations fight wars for it. Yet as you begin to claim it, the only battle for it will be in your own head.

Independence. You're the one who will determine how soon you achieve it, based on what you do and think now.

Nothing Succeeds Like Success

Teenagers need more independence and freedom as they progress through high school. Yet some parents fear the worst, and keep their sons and daughters at home under unrealistically tight rules, with severe restrictions on their social lives. They may have watched too much news or too many talk shows, and they may be alarmed by what they read in the paper or hear about the Internet. It is up to you to begin a march toward your own independence with some honest conversations with your folks.

Your folks are probably very willing to encourage your march toward the independence of adulthood. They may just not be seeing enough signs in you that you are ready to make that march. You can help your folks by showing them a few signs that you deserve their trust.

Remember that most adults aren't expecting you to handle all situations with a lot of maturity and responsibility when you are young. You may be insulted at this little piece of information, but the law—the legal system—considers you immature. That's why all those rules for minors exist.

Many adults may have their doubts about your ability to succeed. However, if you can surprise them every chance you get, you should be able to make them notice you are changing. Instead of showing negative reactions around the house—like pouting, complaining, or trying to get out of all the work you can—do the opposite. You may leave a few mouths open in astonishment, but as you begin carrying your weight at home and acting like a positive force in your family, the message is sure to get through.

Do the same at school. Teachers are used to complaints whenever homework or a test is announced. They're just waiting for a few groans and negative comments. Keep those remarks unsaid a time or two. You'll catch your teachers off guard, and they'll begin to wonder if you really are that "kid" they thought you were, or if you are on the way toward becoming a more positive and realistic individual.

There is one more person you have to convince that you are not a kid anymore—yourself. You will never be able to convince anyone else that you are growing and becoming more responsible unless you believe it first. Think back to all those successes you've had. They'll give you the confidence you need to be more sure of yourself the next time you must move into action. They'll also help you realize that your childhood is a thing of the past.

Try to leave your negative attitude behind, and begin to believe you have something worthwhile to offer others. You can be trusted with their secrets and property. You can handle situations that demand maturity and good sense. You can be counted on! Once you believe in yourself, that belief will radiate to others. Your own confidence in yourself will make others more confident in you. If you act like a champ, you will be a champ. If you act like a loser, don't blame others for thinking you are one.

A Winning Combination

Independence. Maturity. Responsibility. These can be scary words. However, if you can put these three qualities together, you'll be able to get all the freedom you need.

You deserve to be thought of as a capable person. You deserve respect. You deserve recognition for your abilities. Show a bit of these three characteristics, and you'll get what you deserve.

"If I show my parents some independence around the house, they'll kill me," you might say. Maybe. One of the best places to begin to act independently is with your own friends, not at home. Your folks may need to see you handle independence before they start loosening the ties. Let them see it by starting with the people in your group.

Ryan enjoys the outdoors—hiking and doing the nature thing. Over a long weekend, he has the chance to go camping, and he may want to go.

"You're kidding," his pals might say. "Take off to the woods and eat with the mosquitoes when you could be at the concert downtown? You're out of your mind!"

Ryan has two choices. He may not be interested in the group or the music at the concert, and may have no trouble knowing that he really wants to do. His parents know his options, too. They wait and watch. Will Ryan have the independence to do what he wants, or will he give in to peer pressure and go along with the crowd? Sure, he'll have a decent time at the concert, but he'd rather be camping.

If Ryan does what he wants, which in this case isn't hurting anyone, he can prove to himself and to those around him that he is his own person. His friends will enjoy the concert without him, and his folks will begin to understand that Ryan doesn't always follow the crowd. He's showing some strength and independence. By making his own decision, and being comfortable with it, Ryan can take some big steps toward independent living.

Another way you can show independence is by letting people see some leadership. "Me?" you say. "I don't know if I can do it. And besides, when can I get a chance?"

You may baby-sit. You have friends over to the house, and you are involved in different activities. Show some strength once in a while, and suggest new ideas. If you always follow and never show a desire to take the initiative, others won't think you have any sense of independence. There are ways of showing you have a mind of your own without turning people off. You can suggest things without demanding and take charge without being a dictator.

Independence is won, not necessarily just given. Once you prove yourself, you will gain the freedom you want. Give it a try.

Maturity Is a Busy Word!

Maturity doesn't come with age or authority. It is simply using the common sense you have in a responsible way. Acting and reacting with calm, honest sincerity, you can achieve maturity just by being aware of your own worth and the worth of people you meet. That knowledge will give you the confidence to be the leader in major decisions, to listen sincerely to others, and to take on responsibilities that come your way.

Rapping It Up

You deserve the freedom you want. You have a right to it, and in your own time you will get it. The way to obtain freedom is by earning the right to it. By showing some self-assurance, some leadership and independent thinking, and by handling the situations that come along responsibly, you will show people you are ready for even more independence.

There are many characteristics the adult person shows. If you begin to give some hints of them, others will notice you are moving well beyond the "kid" stage. One of those characteristics is an ability to forget about yourself once in a while and think of others. Of course we all think first of ourselves; that's normal. But maturity means knowing how to give. Give others the gift of your sincerity, responsibility, and gratitude. The gift comes back, always. In fact, it comes back with a greater acknowledgment that you are nearing adulthood.

Recognizing the goodness and effort of others is evidence of the growing adult in you. When people give you their best, it would be a sign of maturity for you to show some appreciation. By acknowledging the things people have done for you, you show you are man or woman enough to be aware of their feelings, too. Your friends and the adults in your life who go out of their way for you may often feel unappreciated and forgotten. It's so easy to take people for granted. "That's just part of their job," you might say. But giving genuine concern is never part of a job. It is a sign of unselfish human greatness. Your parents, teachers, and friends have feelings, too. They need some positive reaction once in a while. Make sure those in your life know you think of them as more than simply people who can give you what you want.

No one wants to keep you from growing up. Rather, many people are waiting to see those first signs that show you are on your way. They're waiting for them as they wait for the first flowers of spring. Give them those signs, and you'll notice the difference in their reactions.

The giver always receives. The person who can say a genuine "thank-you" is not only mature, but capable of real human greatness.

Points to Ponder

1. How often do you actually talk in a calm way to the adults in your life, expressing your need for freedom?

_____

How could you do this more effectively?

_____

_____

2. In what area of your life have you matured most during the last year? Be specific and give some examples.

_____

_____

_____

3. Which of your characteristics prevent you from acting more maturely?

_____

_____

How does this happen?

_____

_____

_____

4. In what ways can you improve your sense of responsibility?

_____

_____

_____

Who could help you most in this regard, and how?

_____

_____

Turn Your Dreams into Goals

There's one good thing anyone can say for high school. No matter how grim some days might be or how much pressure, disappointment, or tension you feel, it ends.

"Hurray!" a first- or second-year student might say, "and it won't end one day too soon for me." A junior may take a little more time to come up with the remark. A senior might say it, but there may be a strange lump somewhere deep in his or her throat. Why?

High school has its own set of problems, and you have taken a good look at them as you read this book. There is another dimension of high school, however, that always remains somewhere in the background. It's that sure feeling that whatever is going on now won't last.

High school is just a stepping stone to a long and promising future. As difficult as high school may seem sometimes, at least it becomes familiar to you. You know what others expect of you, you get to know your routine, and things get easier.

The future is uncertain. No matter how hard things seem for you now, there is some feeling of security. At least you know what's going on, even if you may not like it. Psychologists call it a comfort zone. Right now high school and the rest of your life as it exists now is your comfort zone—and they are never easy to leave.

The future is another story. What will you do when you finally get that precious diploma? If you go on to college or move away, how will you leave the friends you've made, and how can you be sure there will be new friends to take their place?

Cliff Notes to Cliff Hangers

"I feel I'm getting ready to jump off a cliff," one senior remarked a few months before graduation. "I've come to the end of the land, and now there's nothing ahead of me but a bunch of clouds and a lot of nothingness. I can't see what's out there, and it's scary."

Of course it can be scary. Moving on is never easy because you can never be sure of what you will find. Even if what has gone before hasn't been that great, at least you knew it, and you could deal with it.

Some teens, on the other hand, look toward the future as an escape. "I can't wait to get out of the house and off on my own. I can't wait to get all these teachers behind me and start doing things my way!"

Sounds good. There's an attitude that seems to creep into these remarks, though, that makes them sound hollow. Remarks such as these are made by teens who feel no satisfaction, happiness, or success in their past or present condition. They think the future is when they will finally be happy. They picture being rich, with a great job—if they need a job at all.

A little hint, though: the future is built on the past, and happiness grows over the years, if it is going to grow at all. True, there should be better years ahead, full of deeper love, richer happiness, and greater satisfaction. That's the way it should be.

But the future isn't an escape. It can't be, because you are taking one big part of the past into it—yourself. Remember the old saying, "Wherever you go, there you are!" Take a little time to realize this. Understand that you don't solve anything by moving away, but only by moving toward something greater and better. How solidly good and rewarding your future will be depends on what you can bring to it from the past—from the *you* that has been.

Have confidence in your future. You take into it that terrific self of yours, that strong, unbeatable will to survive and succeed. Grab hold of it, and don't run away to the future. Run *into* it, and embrace it with all the goodness and love and determination that have been in your life so far. If you can't see that goodness, take another look. It's there. It will make the difference between the future being a repetition of the past, or an exciting time where the thrill of challenge and the search for success make every day unique and full of hope.

What Would You Say?

Write a short piece of advice to students who view the future in the following ways.

1. Kristen has lived in a broken home for years. There are a lot of problems there, but now she has a boyfriend who really cares about her. He doesn't have a good job yet, and Kristen hasn't really decided what she wants to do as a career. But life is so miserable at home that she is considering marriage. At least it would make life better, she says.

_____

_____

_____

_____

2. Steve doesn't think college is the answer for him. He has a chance to work at a local business, and he feels he will be able to advance in this business without a college degree. What would you tell him?

_____

_____

_____

_____

3. Scott and Mandy both want successful careers, but they can't find a university that would offer equally good programs for both of them. Should one give up the chance to get a degree at the best university so they can go to the same school and keep seeing each other?

_____

_____

_____

_____

4. Tammy hasn't been very happy in high school. She really doesn't want to go to college, but she's going to have to do something after graduation. She thinks maybe she'll just keep living at home, get a job as a waitress, and see what happens.

_____

_____

_____

_____

Your Turn

In this space, or on a separate piece of paper, answer these two questions.

1. What do you see yourself doing twenty years from now? Describe your future.

_____

_____

_____

_____

2. How will you make these things happen?

_____

_____

_____

_____

_____

Where's the Goal Line?

Thinking about the future means setting a few goals and making some plans and decisions. Remember, you don't have to plan your whole life during these four years, but it is wise to begin some serious thinking.

Your counselor, your parents, a favorite teacher, or even your friends may help you consider the future. But as you start thinking of an answer to the question, what do I want to be? first resolve to be yourself! Don't fall into the delusion of choosing a career for any other reason than that you think you'll feel fulfilled doing it. Too many young adults go into careers for the money, the prestige, or because they feel it is the hot career of the time. They may end up miserable—stuck in careers that are not comfortable for them. And they may not have enough courage to leave that first line of work and go into something they feel would really be right for them.

If you are a freshman or sophomore, you may have no desire to plan on college at the present. Keep your options open, since you may change your mind before you graduate. If you are a junior or senior, the pressure may seem much more real. At least you can take college entrance tests to find out where you might fit in on the campus scene. You may have underestimated your own ability, and once you realize you are capable of more than you had guessed, you can get the courage to choose a more challenging and satisfying career.

Girls who think they will get married soon after high school and build a family of their own may need to look at some statistics. Four out of every five women eventually live without a marriage partner because of death, divorce, or because they choose the single life. Even for women who are married, the demands of life these days often call for both partners in a marriage to hold jobs. If you don't plan on a career now, you will probably regret it later on. A career can lead to even greater satisfaction and happiness at home. Also, you don't want to run the risk of eventually entering a tight job market with little skills or experience. Think about it. A little training never hurts, and in the long run it is you who must decide not to be hurt by poor planning when you were young.

Your goals may be unclear now, but as you figure them out, keep a calm and realistic eye to the future. Maturity means being able to make responsible decisions, remember? Get all the help you can. Then take an honest look at yourself. Set your goals high, but be realistic, and choose to set yourself on a path that will be comfortable yet challenging for you. Check out your abilities and potential with your counselor, then consider your choices. Leave the daydreams aside, and make your dreams goals. A dream is wishful thinking. A goal is something you can reach with proper planning.

Set some goals for your immediate future after high school. Then give yourself the challenge of more distant goals, too. Life will change, and your goals may change, too. However, if you can at least set yourself in the right direction, you can handle those changes up ahead with confidence in yourself and your abilities.

Dealing with Pressure

The secret to planning for the future lies in being able to handle pressure. Your parents may try to design your future, but don't let them do it. True, they may want you to be a success. Every parent does. But they cannot plan your life for you, because they cannot live your life. Help them realize you are your own person, but also seek their advice. They have had a few more years of experience, and their wisdom can help. However, you should be expected to make the final decisions when it comes to school and career. If your parents make them for you now, you'll never feel you had a chance to begin in a way that was right for you.

Your parents may measure you against older brothers and sisters. If your older brother got a full-time job at eighteen, you shouldn't feel pressured to do the same. If your older sister is in med school, that's great. However, you shouldn't feel it is your duty to follow her there.

The biggest pressure you feel concerning the future may come from inside yourself. How badly do you want success? How about money, prestige, and love? Do you feel you must choose a career that pays the highest salary? Or can you be smart enough to aim for a profession that may not be the most impressive, but one that is right for you?

If you like people, for example, don't bottle yourself up in a profession where contact with others will be limited. You may make good money, but you'll also probably be frustrated after a short time. If you have a hard time dealing with pressure and work yourself into a frenzy until every little thing is perfect, don't choose a career where you will be wrapped up with details for the rest of your life. The more you understand yourself, the greater will be your chance of selecting a profession in which you feel successful, happy, and at peace with yourself.

Where Do I Go from Here?

Life will go on after high school, and the transition won't be as traumatic as you might think. One by one, the puzzle pieces of that first year or two after graduation will fall into place, and you'll begin to see yourself changing. One of the first choices that will help you get a solid feeling about your future is your decision about school. Once you know if and where you are going, getting there doesn't seem quite so frightening.

"Great! So where do I go?"

There may be a few people who are just dying to give you an answer to that one, but right now, they don't matter. *You* matter, and as you try to come to a decision about the future, don't rule out the possibility of more education.

The decision may seem absolutely agonizing right now, but it really isn't. College is not as regimented as high school, and neither are the many trade schools available to young men and women. If you don't want to think about college, check into those schools that teach skills you are interested in developing. The armed forces are another option.

Almost every profession has some training school for future members, and if you need some help finding one, talk to your counselor. If you choose not to consider college, don't choose to stop your education right after high school. There is just too much at stake!

The lure of getting a high-paying job now may tempt you. However, if that job holds no chance for promotion, apprenticeship, or expansion of your talents, it will be a dead end in a few years. A good check may look great to a high school graduate, but it can never replace the long-term value of challenge and preparation for the rest of your life. The world is getting more and more competitive. Few opportunities are available to those who have ended their education with a high school diploma. This is a new century, and society around the world is expecting more from its young adults who enter the work world. You will need more education and more skill development.

If you think college is a possibility—and it is for the great majority of high school graduates—there are some steps you'll need to take to narrow down your choice. Living on campus was once the desired way to go, but now the many junior colleges and local branches of universities provide the option of living at home. At many of these schools, you can work part time while still earning your degree. Local colleges may not offer the expansive sports activities or sprawling campuses of bigger schools, but they are well equipped to prepare students for a range of careers. And they are usually less expensive, which is a big plus for most families.

"No, I need to get out on my own," you might say. Or you may have decided on a career already and know that a university is the best place to prepare you for that field. In that case, your state universities will be the easiest to get into. And while tuition costs are rising everywhere, the state schools will also be the most economical. Private schools tend to cost more, but if you want to attend one of them, they offer a smaller campus and the closeness that is not easily obtained at a large university. Many private schools also have extensive scholarship programs, which you should definitely look into.

Going away for college will give you the opportunity to begin life on your own. It is the first big break from family life, and it will give you a chance to see how well you can decide, manage, and survive without your parents watching every move. At first, all that freedom may be a bit much to handle, but it will show you who you really are. Just be careful of the so-called "party" schools—places where study is not the top priority. There are too many young people now who went overboard with the freedom and wild atmosphere of some schools, and they now have many regrets—and no college diploma.

What School Is Right for Me?

"I need to go to a prestige university." At first, that comment sounds a bit snobby, but the girl who made it wanted to enter a highly competitive career. She knew if she attended one of the premier schools in her field, her chances of working her way to the top were better. Her reasoning was correct.

If your parents can afford it, or if you can get a sufficient scholarship, you may choose to attend a school with prestige and high tuition. Just make sure you have enough valid reasons for doing so. Your parents want the best for you, but you also have the obligation to consider what is reasonable for them. Just check into every scholarship and grant available, because many of these go unused year after year because students are unaware of them or are too lazy to do the necessary paperwork to get the money. Once again, your high school counselor can be a big help here.

Is Marriage for Me?

Marriage is a lifetime commitment. At least that's what it's supposed to be. How far away is it for you? How much do you want it, and how realistically ready are you for it?

Marriage is another big pressure put on many teens after they graduate from high school. If you intend to stay free to pursue a career, or if you just feel you need more time before you give yourself to someone who is worthy of your love and the rest of your life, you'll have to face these decisions realistically. It is possible to have friends of both sexes without making a commitment toward marriage. Believe this, and don't let pressure from others or a feeling of loss drive you into an early marriage for which you may not be ready.

True, that first person who pays special attention to you becomes very precious. He or she may show more love and concern than you may have felt before. Give yourself some time, though, before you promise away your own plans and life. Early marriage may mean fifty or more years of living together. Is being with that person what you really want for all that time?

Sink or Soar?

Leaving high school can seem like jumping off a cliff. Two things can happen once you've made that move. You can sink. Or you can take off into the limitless horizon—free in your spirit and full of confidence in where the wind and your own inner strength can take you.

Which of these two possibilities will be in your future? You can influence your future just by deciding there will be nothing ahead that you can't handle. Admit to yourself that you'll make some mistakes, probably even a big one or two, but you'll make it. Nothing and no one will stop you! You can make your life great by having confidence in yourself.

Don't worry yourself by looking for all the answers. Learn to love the questions, because those questions lead you to the answers. And those answers will be even better than you could ever hope for now. In time, when you are ready, all the answers will come. All you have to do is believe. Never give up on what you always have going for you—yourself, your will to be and to become, your love, and your willingness to live life to its fullest.

Rapping It Up

The future can be scary, if you let it. You may sometimes feel inadequate to handle all its demands. It can beat you down before you even try—if you let it.

But it is possible to face the future. With a little help from counselors, you can get a realistic idea of what career you would like to enter. With some understanding from the people in your life today, you can look forward to meeting new people with different ideas tomorrow. With your own goals set high and your feet on the ground, you can date and really care about someone. You can also choose to wait and promise yourself you'll be sure of someone before you give him or her the rest of your life.

Tomorrow really is an exciting place. It holds new experiences for you. There is happiness ahead you can't even dream of now. There are people who will love the new you that is constantly becoming. The future may hold mystery and uncertainty, but it is yours to challenge and conquer.

A cliff can be the end of the road for those who think they cannot fly. However, for those who trust the wind of time and dare the risk, it can be the beginning of a wonderful new adventure. You *can* soar. You know it, and so do the people who love you. Look ahead. Dare that risk, and go for it all! Your life will only have the limits that you place on it. Brush those last traces of self-doubt away, and the world will open up to you in a thousand different ways.

Points to Ponder

1. What are some hopes you have for the future? Be specific.

_____

_____

_____

2. How will your family members feel when you leave home? Why?

_____

_____

_____

_____

3. How openly can you discuss your plans for the future with your family?

_____

_____

_____

How much support can you expect from them now and in the future?

_____

_____

_____

4. What qualities would you like to see in yourself and your life at the time of your marriage? What would you like your life to look like?

_____

_____

_____

5. What advice would you give a friend who is afraid to face the time after graduation?

_____

_____

_____

You Bet Your Life

So how do you put all this together and make your high school years a roaring success? For starters—and finishers—believe in yourself. With the help of this book, you have taken an honest look at your high school life, and at some things that may be getting in the way of your success. You are beginning to understand that you face challenges and problems. You also, however, know that you have uniqueness and individuality working on your side. You are good. You are intelligent enough to handle what really counts. Believe it!

Be Loyal to Yourself

One of the many talents you possess as a teenager is the ability to spot a fake. You can tell when others are not being sincere, when they are caught up in some cloudy image of what they think they should be, or of what others think they should be.

Take that ability and use it on yourself. If you know who you are, you will also know when you're not being true to yourself.

Take All the Help You Can Get

Because society knows you are a person on the move, it has made all kinds of help available to you. Your folks, your teachers, counselors, and friends are all human, too. If you permit them to know you and share what they have with you, you can gain all the riches they offer. You can make use of their experience, profit from their mistakes, and let them challenge you to new levels of maturity.

You can also help yourself.

Don't be afraid to take those standardized tests the counselors keep talking about. Whether geared to show career possibilities or personality traits, these tests will give you more information and insight on yourself. They can be a big boost toward planning your life. It's true that the test findings should not be taken as absolute truth, but they do provide useful clues to help you plan for the future.

Lead with Your Best Foot Forward

Getting involved in school, church, and neighborhood activities will put you in contact with new situations. Especially if you have felt that life is a bore up to this point, you can begin to find some new areas for exploring your talents. Check over your interest inventory, then look at what's available in your area. Take some initiative. Investigate what's happening in your community, and soon you will find that you've forgotten about old reruns.

You have much to give. There are a lot of people who still don't know that. Let them know. Get out into the world around you and become a caring part of it. That

involvement will not only give you many avenues of
interest and people to add to your life, it will also help you
make a positive impact on the world around you.

Change Is Not a Bad Word

Change is the name of the game—it's the only way you can
progress. One of the surest ways to be comfortable with life
and ward off pressure is simply to realize that whatever
life is, it's always changing.

Many adults develop severe psychological problems
because they need rock-solid security all the time. They
want to get something and then hold onto it. Then when a
new opportunity is available, they're afraid of trying it
because they fear losing what they already have. They
choose to settle for what is safe, are frustrated when any
change happens, and they tend to lead unhappy, clinging
lives.

Our world is changing constantly. The new century has
opened up a floodgate of new potential, in everything from
technology to attitudes. The job you may have when you
are thirty years old may not even be invented yet. Who
knows what life will be like for you in your later years, let
alone in the lives of your children? No one knows what the
future holds.

Scary? Absolutely not! It's very exciting! Realizing the
changes that have already happened in your life can help
you understand your own personal evolutionary process.
By transferring that idea to the rest of the world, and life
in general, you can begin to feel comfortable with change.
You can look forward with eagerness to all those new
things that are still ahead of you.

Be flexible. Be adaptable. Be open. Realize that what is
important to you now may be totally forgotten ten years
from now. Change is not something that is supposed to
give you a nervous breakdown or drive you to depression.
Openness to change will lead to a stronger belief in yourself, and it will give you a more hopeful outlook for the
future.

There Is Nothing Stopping You!

High school is a time for learning. It is also a time for
discovering your own potential. What you learn in the

books is important. But what you gain from knowing yourself and the way you are changing is even more important.

Sometimes teens get depressed by all the things that are happening in their lives. They feel they have too much to handle, and they can't cope with it all. Don't let yourself get frustrated. Learn to put everything in its proper perspective by bringing your values and priorities into play. Just live each day to its fullest, and give your best. What others expect of you must be considered. However, what you expect from yourself will determine how successful you will be and how comfortable you will become with the knowledge of who you really are.

Let the things that can enrich you make your life fuller. Understand and accept the things you cannot change, and be optimistic about your ability to tackle the future. You *can* be a really great human being! If you can learn to forgive the people who may have hurt you, and realize they were acting out of their own ignorance, you can learn to love. If you can respect the humanity and individuality of others, and allow them to be themselves, you will have many friends. If you can live your own life honestly, recognizing your own limitations and your tremendous potential, you can be one of those adults whom other people look to for vision, hope, and example.

Really Rapping It Up

On your graduation day someone will hand you that precious diploma, shake your hand, and say, "Good luck!"

How much luck you really need will depend on how well you succeeded in high school, and how well you use this experience as a stepping-stone to adult life.

You are not defined by your roles.

You are not limited by others' image of you.

You are the one and only, absolutely unique, and potentially terrific—you!

You can take everything that your high school years have to offer and store it neatly away in your own definition of yourself.

Aim high, but realistically.

Live not just as a survivor, but as a successful person— a real champion at the art of living.

Enjoy. Grow. Change. You are a person on the move. So go ahead and move on!

And enjoy your future. You deserve it!